Mindful Mamas and Papas

A Mindful Living Playbook for the *Whole* Family

Sally Jade Powis-Campbell

Archway Publishing books may be ordered through booksellers or by contacting:

Archway Publishing
1663 Liberty Drive
Bloomington, IN 47403
www.archwaypublishing.com
1 (888) 242-5904

Because of the dynamic nature of the Internet, any web addresses or links contained in this book may have changed since publication and may no longer be valid. The views expressed in this work are solely those of the author and do not necessarily reflect the views of the publisher, and the publisher hereby disclaims any responsibility for them.

Any people depicted in stock imagery provided by Getty Images are models, and such images are being used for illustrative purposes only. Certain stock imagery © Getty Images.

This book is a work of non-fiction. Unless otherwise noted, the author and the publisher make no explicit guarantees as to the accuracy of the information contained in this book and in some cases, names of people and places have been altered to protect their privacy.

ISBN: 978-1-4808-7101-4 (sc)
ISBN: 978-1-4808-7103-8 (hc)
ISBN: 978-1-4808-7102-1 (e)

Library of Congress Control Number: 2019930780

Print information available on the last page.

Archway Publishing rev. date: 3/27/2019

This book goes to our littles.
Those on earth for our daily adventures, our babe who found a cozy place in our hearts to join us on those adventures, and perhaps other babes who may come into our lives. Without you, there'd be no mindful mama or papa. You teach us, challenge us, and bring us into the present moment, no matter what that moment has in store.

Contents

Pause, Mamas and Papas

The demands of life often impact our ability to practice patience and compassionate listening with our children. This can affect the quality of our parent-child relationships. Lack of awareness and attention may lead to a buildup of frustration and confusion for both parents and children. By pausing to identify reactive patterns, bringing mindful awareness into our daily lived lives, and exploring options for attending to life's many stressors, you can improve your ability to respond skillfully to your own needs and the needs of your children and partner.

Before you get in the mindful parenting game, let's pause, mamas and papas. As a working mom with toddlers and part-time childcare, I get that "pausing" is easier said than done. If your intention is to be more mindful, rest assured: Pausing is part of the process. So well done—by just taking this moment to pause, you're already on the mindful parenting team.

It's a good team to be on. It saved my marriage and has brought more joy into every day routine activities with my children and husband. It's not that I'm hitting the "Like" button on every moment of parenthood—because I'm certainly not. I'm now noticing little glimmers of connection, tapping into the senses, and experiencing gratitude for the gifts from Mother Earth and my family members.

You've got this; mindfulness is your way.

The Imperfect Practice

Let's get one thing straight: This book isn't about being on a soapbox telling you how to be the perfect parent. Because *that* I certainly am not. We'll be throwing the concept of "perfect parent," "perfect kid," "perfect (insert any other unattainable role for perfection)" out with the bathwater as we take this mindfulness journey together.

Parenting is a wonderful mix of joy, worry, laughter, stress, play, frustration, tenderness, chaos, and everything in between, aptly described by Jon Kabat-Zinn as "the full catastrophe of parenting." Creating moments of stillness to reconnect with ourselves and reflect on our parenting can be a challenge, but it can also be hugely rewarding as we navigate this full catastrophe. Again, mindful parenting is not about somehow becoming the perfect parent; it's about being present in our parenting, with all its imperfections.

Your Mindful Parenting Coaches

At this point, you may be wondering who I am and why you should hear me out. I'm a mama, first and foremost, who has experienced the wild game of parenting firsthand, while juggling roles as a psychologist, yoga teacher, meditation guide, wife, public speaker, competitive athlete, and entrepreneur.

So where does "author" fit in?

I'll take you back a few years (or decades) to when I was in diapers. It wasn't long after that I was planning my future role as a mama, collecting baby names in lock-and-key journals and practicing creations in the kitchen to feed my fictitious family (those Cabbage Patch Dolls were my intro to picky eaters). I trained to be a mama all my life, it seems. It wasn't socialization; it was passion and a love for adventure.

Insert many years of schooling, backpacking across countries, and mental health challenges as a young woman growing up with the pressures of media and then *social* media.

Jon, who is now my husband, and I met in 2009; we were both content in our single lives as students working toward our master's degrees. We met one night at a literal fork in a road in Kensington, a neighborhood in Calgary, Alberta. Little did we know the meaning of that. Our date started as a casual after-work bite and pint at an Irish pub, which led to a walk along the river, ice cream in a park, and walking to yet another park to sit on a bench and talk until the stars came out to light our walk back to that fateful fork in the road, where we had parked. We shared a tender kiss at that fork in the road, and I remember it so vividly to this day. Six months later, we went on a trip to Seattle, visiting Pike Place Market, and found a vintage jewelry seller with a one-of-a-kind ring that suited us perfectly. Jon wanted some tradition, so he held onto that ring until the next time we happened to be near that fork in the road. As we passed the fork in the road, you guessed it: he got down on one knee.

We got married in his parents' backyard to the backdrop of the majestic Rocky Mountains (and a whole lot of rain that day). For the next year, we focused our energies on traveling as much as we could, while it was just the two of us, and creating a life. We shared life experiences that have brought us to here, before you, sharing our words and plays.

Oops, I Stopped Breathing

It wasn't as easy as we expected to create said life, but with the assistance of fertility treatments and alternative support in the forms of chiropractic, acupuncture, and yoga therapy, we made a little babe. While pregnant with our first, it seemed as though I was focused on my breath all the time.

I completed a thirty-day yoga challenge, enrolled in a mindfulness-based professional development course, and attended a nine-week natural birthing course with Jon. I was intent on nourishing my mind and body as well as that of my growing baby, whom I had yearned for all my life. As I was in the midst of a natural home birth, my journey into motherhood came with some bumps in the road. Namely, my sweet baby got stuck in the birth canal, requiring a trip to the hospital for an emergency C-section.

Like so much else in my life to that point, I couldn't control all aspects of this parenting gig the day I became a mother. But this reflection didn't come until six months postpartum; I was running down a path with my babe in the stroller, on autopilot, mind scurrying from one thought to the next. Then it dawned on me: up until the birth of my sweet boy, *all* I focused on was my breath. One whole cycle at a time: inhale, pause, exhale, pause, repeat. Fast-forward to six months postpartum: I felt as though I was gasping for air as I drowned in dirty laundry, cloth diapers, parenting books, and homemade baby purées. I was wading from one play date to the next, all in this pursuit of perfect motherhood. I wasn't breathing. At that point, I didn't know where to reach for my oxygen mask so I could help myself, let alone help my partner and child.

I got home and started writing. It started with these two words: "Breathe, Mama."

I've been writing ever since that day in spring 2014. This book is my other baby that has crawled and scrawled and is ready to enter the world (no emergency surgery necessary).

Playbook Use

Consider this book as a playbook, not a textbook that gathers dust (and guilt) on your bedside table. No, no. This book contains all the plays you can consider implementing into your mindful parenting game. *The Mindful Mamas and Papas* is served up in sections: "Breathe," "Meditate," "Create," "Move and Play," and "Eat and Drink." We can infuse mindful play into all these practices on a daily basis. You can flip this playbook open to any page and find a coaching for solo, partner, or family activities.

Along with many activities, I'll offer up fun easily digested facts, tips for how you can take an activity to the next level, and resources for further exploration if you enjoyed the activity. Just look for these notes:

History: Fun historical facts about the practices or foods featured.
Science: Research on topics or practices.
Upgrade: Extra skills or ingredients you can add on to meditations, crafts, or recipes.
Explore: Resources on given page topic, such as apps, books, or websites.

Throughout this book, you'll find stunning color images, but you'll also find black-and-white illustrations in each section and empty frames accompanying some recipes. No, these aren't just signs of a forgetful mama. We want you to be playful and have your family members color and doodle away in the illustrations. We also know how popular taking photos of food creations are these days, so try out a recipe, take a snap, upload it to your local drugstore for printing, and glue it onto the page of the recipe. Share your doodles and photos on Instagram by tagging @mindfulmamasandpapas.

You'll also find quotes throughout this book. In grade 7, I began writing quotes in a notebook. A couple years later, I entered all the quotes in a computer document, and I'm still adding to that document today. In this book, I've included a few quotes that have made me stop in my tracks as a human, a friend, a mom, a partner, and all the other roles I play. I hope that some of these strike a chord for you, or at the very least, you come to the realization how powerful words are that have mindful intention behind them.

Now that's *how* you use this playbook. But *who* should use it? It was particularly important to Jon and me to write this book for moms *and* dads seeking to experience the benefits of mindfulness in their daily lives. Right now, there are plenty of mindfulness books for moms. But what about the dads out there? The biggest feedback I hear when I run my community-based Mommy Mindfulness and Moms Who Meditate classes is that it's all well and good for moms to get these skills, but if they're not being practiced by both parents, parenting can feel more like an individual chore than a team sport. So I started hosting Mindful Mamas and Papas events, with great response from the community.

Finding Your Flow

What I love about hosting mindful parenting sessions in the community is hearing about when parents start to experience flow state more often by integrating some of the activities included in this book. Maybe you recall a recent time when you were fully engaged, present, and finding sparks of joy in the moment with your family. You could say this was your flow state. It's a contrast to those times when you're only focusing on the crowd at a grocery store, watching your screaming toddler, hearing criticisms from yourself or others for your child's behavior, and other times you don't feel in the moment but are rather considering how your turf is less than green compared to another family's field.

Mindfulness practice doesn't make the perfect parent, but practice increases your odds of getting into flow, that state when whatever you're doing feels almost effortless, even in challenging circumstances. Mindfulness is a *practice* that you can cultivate daily to help you find that flow.

Practice (Over) Perfection

It bears repeating: perfection is unattainable. Mindfulness, on the other hand, is something everyone (Yes, even you) can cultivate through practices in this book. At the core of mindfulness are the values of nonstriving, nonjudgment, and noncomparison. So the next time playground parent small talk has you feeling weak, imperfect, or less of a parent, let it goooooo with your next exhale. We often see someone's highlight reel on social media; we rarely see the behind-the-scenes fumbles.

Practicing being present in the game of life is key to being more *responsive* rather than *reactive* with your family, to lifting some of the weight that comes with parenting off your shoulders.

Executing on game day is key. Those days when you have an overworked and under-rested partner, cranky toddler, or moody teen pushing every last button. You have no choice but to get in the game. You have to be on. You must practice the play (such as mindful breathing and meditation) not first in this stressed time. Instead, bring intention and commitment to make it to your practice daily. Practice in times and spaces that are conducive your family life.

A weekend warrior mentality seems to be where many parents have found themselves in today's world. No, I'm not telling you to quit your day job if you have one. What I am suggesting is that you use one mindfulness practice a day to easily integrate into your family's routine, not just cram a family yoga class into a Saturday morning and outdoor walk Sunday morning, and go on autopilot the other five days of the week. One must cultivate mindfulness in a slow and steady fashion. You don't just practice it on the bad days when you're feeling stressed, depressed, overwhelmed, or anxious. Doing it regularly can help slow you down, so you can enjoy the moment, and assist you when things become challenging.

It's about playing smarter, not harder. The more you develop your mindful parenting skill set, the easier and more enjoyable the parenting game becomes.

Pause, Then Parent (and Play)

Rest and recovery are key to athletics and parenthood alike. Recreational and pro athletes work periods of rest into their routine. This rest, or pause, gives time for reflecting on plays or skills to work on. In the same way we need to rest in athletics, parents need time-outs too. Self-imposed time-outs may be called for. Also, as you start integrating more mindful activities into the home, your children will start to point out when you need to breathe or meditate.

Rest benefits both physical and mental health for parents. It's a chance for you to leave the game, even for just a run or a wine night with friends, and come back refreshed. Your nervous system is in a stressed state when always on the go. We rarely rest our nervous system. You need to treat your mental health like athletes do their muscles.

How? Simple. Sit. Notice your thoughts, body sensations, and emotional state. Or in other words, meditate where it fits into your routine, but the key is to make it part of your routine. In *The Tools of Titans*, Timothy Ferris notes more than 80 percent of the two hundred world-class performers he interviewed had some form of daily meditation or mindfulness practice. I get it; pausing as a parent is easier said than done, and pro athletes or CEOs are likely to have assistants, nannies, and money to support them in finding pause. But you can find space and time daily for one activity in this book, I assure you. It may mean building a doable routine, creating boundaries to protect it, and asking others for support in doing so (turn to pages 11-15 to get your routine started).

Be Mindful of Your Coach and Teammates

In sports, everyone has a coach and teammates. Your team has to be on the same page. This is where mindful partnering comes in. Whether parents are together or apart, or if you're partnering with caregivers in your community, a team approach to raising children supports everyone.

The best athletes in the world have coaches. It's not something to be ashamed of. To tackle this parenting game alone or with just your partner won't get you any awards. I have coaches and a support network I can ask for advice or try out ideas on and accept guidance from in my professional and parenting roles, and it's been invaluable.

Mindful Parenting and Partnering

Mindful Parenting and Partnering: Introduction

• • • • • • • • • • • • • • •

The Birth and Growth of Mindfulness

While mindfulness practice grew out of Buddhism thousands of years ago, it's recently become a popular concept—and not just with yogis. Mindfulness is increasingly accepted and studied in the worlds of science, health care, education, business, the military, and athletics, as well as parenting and relationships.

What Is Mindfulness?

Mindfulness is the practice of deliberately paying attention in the present moment. It involves being fully aware of what's happening both inside—in your body, heart, and mind—and outside yourself, in your environment. Using your senses—sight, smell, taste, touch, hearing, and awareness of thought—can increase awareness of your own internal forecast as well as your children or partner's disposition. Mindfulness is awareness without judgment or criticism. Mindfulness brings to us practices to emphasize gratitude and self-compassion.

Mindful awareness doesn't just happen overnight—especially if you're at the stage of parenthood where those nights are generally sleepless. One must cultivate mindfulness in a slow and steady fashion. You don't just practice it on the bad days, when you're feeling stressed, overwhelmed, or anxious.

Doing mindfulness exercises regularly can help slow you down and can assist you in helping your child (and partner) build more mindful awareness. It's key to get the practice down *yourself* in order to teach it. It's kind of like securing your own oxygen mask first on an airplane before helping others. You're in a place to better support and take care of others around you—children, partners, friends, and colleagues.

What Are Mindfulness Practices?

Formal mindfulness practices include sitting meditation, body scan meditation, and even walking meditation. Meditations can be relatively brief—as little as five minutes—but can also be practiced in a more intensive manner for extended durations. The informal practice of mindfulness can occur while running, snowboarding, cleaning, knitting, reading, or tapping into your senses to have a mindful sip of coffee in the morning. These informal practices sprinkled through your day help you generalize mindful awareness to everyday life.

Why Should Families Practice Mindfulness?

Our children are growing up in a time much different from the one we grew up in. More and more, they are experiencing stress, overwhelmed feelings, and related uncomfortable states. If parents nurture mindfulness from early childhood, it may foster greater resilience within families and encourage everyone in the family to refine their own mindfulness practice. For children, this practice provides a skillful way for them to relate to life's challenging moments.

You may have heard the anecdotal evidence of the benefits of mindfulness practice from magazines, office cooler chats, or yoga classes. But there's some hard science on the effectiveness of mindfulness. Bringing mindfulness into parenting is a truly valuable application of the practice. Mindful parenting interventions are increasingly being used to help attend to parenting problems, prevent and treat mental disorders in children, and remediate intergenerational transmission of mental disorders from parents to children.

Paying attention to your life, here and now, with kindness and curiosity.
—*Amy Saltzman*

Incorporating meditation, mindful breathing, mindful eating, yoga, and other mindfulness-based activities and formal mindfulness-based interventions have been found to

- reduce stress (Goyal et al. 2014);
- enhance self-control and reduce reactivity for all ages (Bishop et al. 2004; Masicampo and Baumeister 2007; Ortner et al. 2007);
- enhance concentration, mental clarity, and focus among adults (Young 1997) as well as in children with ADHD (Moore and Malinowski 2009; Zhang et al. 2016);
- reduce conduct and anger management problems among children and teens (Burke 2009);
- enhance emotional intelligence (Walsh and Shapiro 2006);
- mitigate the effects of bullying on children (Zhou et al. 2016);
- improve children's and adults' capacity to respond with kindness, compassion, and acceptance of others (Fulton 2005; Wallace 2001);
- improve children's academic performance and emotional development (Schonert-Reichl et al. 2015);
- reduce anxiety, from childhood through adulthood (Cristiano et al. 2016; Hofmann et al. 2010);
- reduce attention problems (Crescentini et al. 2016);
- improve social skills when taught to children and adolescents (Schonert-Reichl et al. 2015);

- help parents manage stress more effectively (Goyal et al. 2014); mindful parenting programs in particular have been found to reduce parental stress and the resulting parental reactivity (Bogels, Lehtohnen, and Restifo 2010);
- increase quality of sleep (Burke 2009);
- protect against the emotionally stressful effects of relationship conflict (Barnes et al. 2007);
- boost mindful responding in couples, such as listening without taking things personally or overreacting (Block-Lerner et al. 2007);
- bring awareness to the destructive thought patterns that undermine relationships and reduce marital conflicts (Molajafar et al. 2015);
- enhance intimacy (Lazaridou and Kalogianni 2013);
- combat the inevitable routine of long-term relationships and boost relationship satisfaction (Barnes et al. 2007; Wachs and Cordova 2007); and
- help sustain emotional and physical connectedness between parents and children at a time of parents' divorce (Altmaier and Maloney 2007).

What Is Mindful Parenting?

Learning to be a mindful parent means paying attention to how your body, mind, and emotions respond to routine, challenging, and joyous events in your life: in your *whole* life, in which you flow between your roles as a partner, parent, cleaner, athlete, chef, volunteer, teacher, creator, friend, employee, entrepreneur.

Ensure you're performing to the very best of your abilities in all your roles by leaving mindless thought wandering behind and allowing your body and mind to work together with combined physical and mental focus. The informal practices of mindfulness are where the magical mindful moments for parents can be found. Think the first mindful cup of hot coffee (okay, let's be real; the first mindful sip is where we'll start). Or consider how to be mindful during a spin class or on a run with your running stroller. With the mindful practices and crafting in this book, you'll be putting play and pause in your parenting gig in no time (or now time).

What Is Mindful Partnering?

Mindfulness is about *intentionality*. At the beginning of a relationship, in the honeymoon phase, sharing is a natural process. You want to know everything: what your new love is thinking about moment to moment, what he or she wants to do in life, what brings him or her joy. With mindfulness comes the possibility of renewing that sense of curiosity about your relationships, food, nature, and routine daily activities, such as your morning cup of coffee. As noted earlier, there is hard science showing that mindfulness can benefit you and your partner.

But reaping those benefits takes some commitment. Mamas and papas, I know it can be challenging taking time from the many to-dos on your list to ask your partner for what you want and need. There are exercises in this book to encourage you to do this, because if you don't ask for it, your partner or other childcare providers may have a very hard time knowing what it is that you actually want and need. Likewise, we're often so focused on our children that we get out of touch with our partner, which is where exercises for boosting partner attunement come in, such as joint breathing exercises.

Mindful partnering includes everything from fighting fair to making it a priority to have time together to talk with your partner. We've all felt the stresses and disconnection that come on. We feel like ships passing in the night while juggling all that comes with family and work and play in life.

The intention of this book is first and foremost to support *you*, mamas and papas, to support you in being more present in parenting and partnering, to find more pause and play in the everyday. This is not to just add one more thing to your to-do list.

What are your intentions for picking up this book and for mindfulness practice in your life?

Leverage the science-backed tools of intention setting to build more self-awareness, closeness with your partner, and closeness with your children. Research on intention setting in sports, business, psychology, and other fields suggests that clarifying what you want and putting it out there helps you create it.

The first step in mindfulness is about making a choice to pay attention to something. To meet you where you're at, this playbook offers up an intention-setting worksheet for you to dive deep to the roots of what underlies your attention and inattention to relationships, tasks, and even this book. Intentions support family members in discovering more about the world, each other, and themselves. Now is the time to bring pause and presence to your family's mindfulness journey, no matter where you are on that path.

Mindful Parents in a Modern Village

In the modern world, families don't fit into a mold. There are many people raising children: moms, dads, stepparents, grandparents, and nannies. To not acknowledge the beautiful array of family structures would be a disservice (and not very mindful). As such, the intention-setting worksheets are created for your family no matter its shape, size, and makeup—mamas, papas, stepparents, grandparents, foster parents, and beyond.

Set the Scene for Mindful Parent Intention Setting

Before you engage in this intention-setting exercise, make space within you and around you. Find a space where you can pour your mind, body, and heart into the experience. This may mean asking for support, locking a door, lighting a candle, and doing what it takes to help you feel grounded.

> **Upgrade:** Flip to the "Breathe" section to choose a breathing exercise to come to your breath and the present moment before setting your intentions.

Now give yourself the gift of time—a minimum of ten minutes—to explore questions intended to support you in setting the intention for mindfulness for you and your family. Don't overthink your answers, strive for the right response, or judge or criticize yourself. Allow the answers to flow from you in the here and now.

> **Explore:** You can download this template from the book's web page. This is great if you are a two-parent household, if you want pages for grandparents or stepparents, or if you want to revisit or redo this intention-setting exercise monthly, annually, or every other year.

Mindful Mama Intention Setting

- Mindfulness is _____
  _____

- Being a mom is _____
  _____

- Mindful parenting is _____
  _____

- I want to practice mindfulness because _____
  _____

- If I am more mindful, I will _____
  _____

- Mindfulness could support me in my role as a parent by _____
  _____

- Mindfulness could support me in my role as a partner by _____
  _____

- Parenting activities I'm most mindful during are _____
  _____

- Partnering activities I'm most mindful during are _____
  _____

- Parenting activities I do mindlessly, on autopilot, are _____
  _____

- Partnering activities I do mindlessly, on autopilot, are _____
  _____

- Areas I need support in are _____
  _____

Now ask your partner or your parent (your child's grandparent) the following:

- In what ways do you see me flourishing as an individual and as a parent? _____
  _____

- In what ways do you see me struggling as an individual and as a parent? _____
  _____

Read and reflect on your answers. This exercise helps you clarify your motivations and intentions of mindfulness. When defining your mindful intention below, consider what you want you and your family to stand for, appreciate, and value. An intention doesn't have to be an extravagant statement; make it as fun and exciting as you want. An intention is the starting point of every dream, and it's nourished by creativity that can fulfill all your needs in the roles you play.

My mindful parenting intention is _____
_____

Whatever intention you choose to set, now is the perfect time to do so. It's also good to look back at your answers above if you need motivation to meditate or would like to create a new intention.

Let's dig deeper and set ritual intentions. These are consistent, repetitive events or actions you want to be part of your and your family's life. Examples:

- going to a yoga class every Sunday night to restore and recharge
- creating a feel-good playlist and listening to it while folding laundry one day per week
- getting outside with my child for twenty minutes daily on weekdays after work or school

    - A consistent ritual I intend to integrate into my self-care practice is _____
    _____

    - A consistent ritual I intend to bring into my family's life is_____
    _____

Next, set *implementation intentions*, which enable parents to translate good intentions into action. Implementation intentions identify where, when, and how you'll implement actions so it's more likely you'll be true to your parenting intentions. Just explore behaviors or actions that don't support you in being present or tapping into your intentions. You create implementation intentions with the simple formula "when X happens, I'll do Z." Examples:

- "When I yell at a family member for not getting enough me time, I'll apologize for raising my voice and ask for a time-out to review the family calendar and choose a time slot to do an activity solo."
- "When my child has a tantrum or other challenging behavior, I'll put on soothing music, put on a candle or diffuser, and make a cup of tea to help me find calm."
- "When I first see my partner at the end of a work day or day with the kids, I'll tell my partner something that made me smile today."

    - Actions I intend to integrate into my self-care practice: _____
    _____

    - Actions I intend to bring into my family's life: _____
    _____

Mindful Papa Intention Setting

- Mindfulness is _____
  _____

- Being a dad is _____
  _____

- Mindful parenting is _____
  _____

- I want to practice mindfulness because _____
  _____

- If I am more mindful, I will _____
  _____

- Mindfulness could support me in my role as a parent by _____
  _____

- Mindfulness could support me in my role as a partner by _____
  _____

- Parenting activities I'm most mindful during _____
  _____

- Partnering activities I'm most mindful during _____
  _____

- Parenting activities I do mindlessly, on autopilot, are _____
  _____

- Partnering activities I do mindlessly, on autopilot, are _____
  _____

- Areas I need support in are _____
  _____

Now ask your partner or your parent (your child's grandparent) the following:

- In what ways do you see me flourishing as an individual and as a parent? _____
  _____

- In what ways do you see me struggling as an individual and as a parent? _____
  _____

Read and reflect on your answers. This exercise helps you clarify your motivations and intentions of mindfulness. When defining your mindful mama/papa intention below, think deeply about what you want yourself as a parent or your family to stand for, appreciate, and value. An intention doesn't have to be an extravagant statement; make it as fun and exciting as you want. An intention is the starting point of every dream and is nourished by creativity that can fulfill all your needs in the roles you play.

My mindful parenting intention is _____
_____

Whatever intention you choose to set, now is the perfect time to do so. It's also good to look back at your answers above if you need motivation to meditate or would like to create a new intention.

Let's dig deeper and set ritual intentions. These are consistent, repetitive events or actions you want to be part of your and your family's life. Examples:

- going to a yoga class every Sunday night to restore and recharge
- creating a feel-good playlist and listening to it while folding laundry one day per week
- getting outside with your child for twenty minutes after work or school

    - A consistent ritual I intend to integrate into my self-care practice is _____
      _____

    - A consistent ritual I intend to bring into my family's life is _____
      _____

Next, set implementation intentions, which enable parents to translate good intentions into action. Implementation intentions identify where, when, and how you'll implement actions so it's more likely you'll be true to your parenting intentions. Just explore behaviors or actions that don't support you in being present or tapping into your intentions. You create implementation intentions with the simple formula "When X happens, I'll do Z." Examples:

- "When I yell at a family member for not getting enough me time, I'll apologize for raising my voice and ask for a time-out to review the family calendar and choose a time slot to do a solo activity."
- "When my child has a tantrum or other challenging behaviors, I'll put on soothing music, put on a candle or diffuser, and make a cup of tea to help me find calm."
- "When I first see my partner at the end of a work day or day with the kids, I'll tell my partner something that made me smile today."

    - Actions I intend to integrate into my self-care practice: _____
      _____
      _____

    - Actions I intend to bring into my family's life: _____
      _____
      _____

The benefits of mindfulness practice include stress reduction. This is a reason many parents come into my practice. Parenting and partnering are roles rife with stress. Conflict, loss, and overcommitment are common causes of stress. Stress is the body's response to stressful situations. Here, we go beyond intention setting and digging down deep into your experience of stress and perhaps a life lived on autopilot. Let's brainstorm the causes of stress in your life and build coping mechanisms to support you. It can be helpful to look at how you experience and cope with stress at present and choose tools you'll learn all about in this book to help you out. You can find this *Mind Your Stress* template on the book's website; have your partner and yourself complete it or revisit it again yourself after a period of practicing mindfulness regularly.

What causes your stress? List the things you found stressful over the past month:

_____

_____

What about chronic stresses? List the biggest causes of stress for you over the past year or longer:

_____

_____

Your Experience of Stress

Stress can result in problematic symptoms, especially when experienced over an extended period of time. How do you know when you're in a stressed state? What are the initial thoughts, body sensations, and emotions when you experience stress? Look at the following physical symptoms of stress and circle those you regularly experience:

- headaches
- back pain
- neck pain
- problems with digestion
- nausea
- shaking
- sweating
- dizziness
- numbness or tingling
- chest pain or discomfort
- other pain or discomfort

Look at the following emotional, behavioral, and cognitive symptoms of stress and circle those you regularly experience:

- burnout
- decreased productivity
- concentration problems
- memory problems
- crying

- frustration
- confusion
- irritability
- impatience
- emotional fatigue

How You Cope with Stress

What are your current stress management techniques?

_____

_____

How effective are these stress management techniques for you?

_____

_____

Switching up Your Stressful Situations

Now choose a source of stress below or identify one you'd like to improve:

- partner or child relationship challenges
- lack of social support
- overcommitment
- grief and loss

Stressful situation:

_____

_____

Now take a moment to consider how the stressful situation you noted above can be improved. Examples below:

- Partner or child relationship challenges: "This situation can be improved with assertive communication training, setting boundaries, reducing technology use, and resolving the conflict."

- Lack of social support: "This situation can be improved with calling new or old friends instead of texting, asking one person for support per week or month, or joining a club or group with common interests."

- Overcommitment: "This situation can be improved with practicing saying no, setting boundaries, reducing time, or completely eliminating some things from my schedule."

- Grief and loss: "This situation can be improved with seeking support from friends, family, or professionals; journaling; or finding enjoyable activities to fill my day."

How can your stressful situation be improved?

_____

_____

Curating Coping Strategies for Stress

You're a parent; stress is going to happen in your life. Having a variety of stress management tools in your self-care kit is key. Choose some tools and practice them regularly to boost the likelihood of stopping stress from building up and experiencing the symptoms of stress you noted earlier.

Here are some examples of healthy coping strategies to practice with the intention of reducing stress and the impact it has on you emotionally, physically, behaviorally, and cognitively:

- meditating
- yoga
- journaling
- coloring
- painting
- knitting
- deep breathing
- self-massage
- mindful eating habits
- exercising
- bathing
- walking (solo or with the entire family, a partner, friends, or colleagues)
- creating and listening to a feel-good playlist
- playing a musical instrument

List two coping strategies you've used in the past and would like to use more regularly:

_____
_____

List two new coping strategies listed above that you would like to try:

_____
_____

When and where will you use these coping strategies?

_____
_____
_____
_____

It's important to create boundaries to support your use of the four coping strategies you've chosen. You'll need a dedicated space and time, which may mean asking partners or making childcare arrangements to have this uninterrupted self-care time. How will you create your boundaries?

_____
_____
_____
_____
_____
_____

Mindful Parenting and Partnering: Mindful Tools

• • • • • • • • • • • • • •

There are a number of tools for practicing mindfulness referenced in this book. Now, this can't be said enough: You don't need anything fancy to practice mindfulness. However, there are household products or easy-to-procure items to support your family's mindfulness practices.

Essential Oils

You can purchase 100 percent essential oils from most grocery stores and pharmacies. However, visiting a local apothecary can be a great treat for children and teens. Tap into your senses and learn the mental and physical health benefits of these plant-based products. Consult health care practitioners and manufacturers' claims to learn their proper use, precautions, and drug interactions. You can also purchase mini vials to hand-make essential oil blends for your family.

> **Science**: Essential oils offer far greater power than simply making a room smell nice. Research has shown that some essential oils are calmative and relieve GI discomfort, headaches, and skin irritations.

Yoga Mats and Meditation Seating

These are great for the obvious, yoga practice, but you can also roll them up and place them under your tailbone for a seated meditation practice. For meditation seating, you can use a kitchen chair or couch. You can also support yourself on the floor with the use of a rolled-up towel, meditation cushion, rolled yoga mat, or bolster. For those looking to invest further, you can purchase a special meditation bench or get a woodworking family member or friend to create one for you.

Journal and Writing Supplies

It can be a mindful activity in and of itself to visit a local shop to hand-pick a journal for you and your family members. You may choose blank pages, lined pages, or even pages that have gratitude practice prompts. Likewise picking pens and pencils. There are so many colors out there. I recently visited a major department store with my two toddlers, and we spent forty-five minutes in the stationery aisle alone. Don't rush; have a conversation on what type of writing utensil you are attracted to: is it the color, the shape, the size? You don't need ten pens, but find a special one for your journal. This can also be a kid-free mindful activity for mamas or papas to grab a coffee and wander through a local shop slowly, silently, and mindfully.

Sound

You can download apps that have a mindful sound, such as Insight Timer, which offers timer sound options including singing bowls, wooden blocks, and more. Or you can invest in a beautiful Tibetan singing bowl or set of chimes. Many towns have yoga studios or meditation shops that sell these products, or you can purchase them online.

Mala Beads

For some, the sight of mala beads around the neck or lying on a meditation cushion can serve as a reminder to meditate. Many who have malas use them to recite a mantra while meditating. Malas come in varying sizes, and there are a wide variety of materials to choose from. You may choose to make your own using the instructions provided in this playbook (pages 126-127).

Phone and Tablet Apps

If you're looking for mindfulness on the go or a support for your mindfulness at home, you can download apps by simply searching some of the following terms:

- yoga apps (examples include *Pocket Yoga, Yoga.com Studio, 5 Minute Yoga, Kids' Yoga Deck, Super Stretch Yoga*)

- guided breathing and meditation apps and timers for silent meditation (examples include *Calm, Headspace, Insight Timer, Meditation Oasis*)

- kids' mindfulness apps (examples include *Breathe Think Do Sesame, DreamyKid, Calm Counter, Calm, Breathing Bubbles*)

- mindful eating apps (for example, *Eat Right Now*)

Or look on YouTube for mindfulness videos (examples include *Thich Nhat Hanh's 10 Mindful Movements* or *Cosmic Kids Yoga*).

Other Mindful Tools

- bubbles
- blankets
- stuffed animals
- stones, twigs, flowers
- candles (battery-powered or nontoxic regular candles)
- Hoberman sphere

Mindful Crafting Supplies

By no means an exhaustive list, but below is a list of some of the supplies you can collect from nature or local shops for the activities included in the "Create" section of this book.

- mason jars
- used plastic bottles
- paper plates
- yarn, string
- natural materials (stones, twigs, pine cones, shells, dried plant parts, sand)
- nontoxic glue
- glitter
- nontoxic dish soap
- nontoxic paint
- beads
- essential oil vials
- recycled and washed glass jars
- shea butter
- olive oil
- essential oils
- cream of tartar
- salt
- all-purpose flour
- nontoxic food dye
- pencils and crayons
- markers
- stickers
- scissors
- fabric scraps
- tape
- crochet doilies
- paper

Mindful Parenting and Partnering: Being Mindful of Your Audience

• • • • • • • • • • • • • •

Mindfulness is for all ages, but some activities or ways of approaching mindful practices are more suited to particular ages. This is a quick guide on catering to the practitioners.

Adapting Mindfulness Activities for Kids

There are a number of tools and strategies in this book that are appropriate for specific age groups. But it's useful to know how to adapt adult breathing and meditation exercises for younger ones. Here are a few tips:

- Keep it short, starting with thirty seconds and slowly increasing time frame.

- Keep it simple; keep instructions and number of tools used to a minimum.

- Customize for your family and your setting.

- Use play, activities, and movement skills.

- Have fun and keep a healthy sense of humor in the practice.

- Demonstrate each skill for a given activity, then do it together, and progressively fine-tune the child's practice.

Making Mindfulness Skills Relevant for Teens

Here are a few ways to rationalize and adapt adult mindfulness activities for a teen audience:

- Keep mindfulness practices short, at around ten minutes, and gradually increase time frame.

- Use music suited to the teens' taste to practice mindful listening skills.

- Use walking, yoga, and other movement mindfulness skills.

- Share world leaders—from athletes to scientists to CEOs—who practice mindfulness to enhance their performance in personal and professional endeavors.

- Support them in integrating mindfulness practice into daily routine activities, including brushing teeth, showering, walking, eating, studying, texting, listening to music, practicing sports, and more.

Mindful Parenting and Partnering: Man-Tras and Mom-Tras

• • • • • • • • • • • • • •

As a parent, you're used to listening to the same things over and over and over and over again: "I don't want to eat that. I don't like it. I don't want to eat it." And it's not just toddlers we're talking about here. Children of all ages and partners can push our buttons.

Repeating a mantra to myself has helped me soothe and clear my mind many times and in various situations. These short and rhythmic repetitions, when practiced regularly, have supported me in harnessing inner strength and finding footing in the present, often right about the time I feel like I'm falling apart at the seams as a mom.

I introduce thoughts for mantras for parents (Jon refers to them as "man-tras" and "mom-tras"). The literal definition of *mantra* is "set free the mind." The dictionary definition for *mantra* is "instrument of thought."

In Buddhism, one of the many purposes of mantras is to aid in concentration, mindfulness, and meditation. For parents, mantras can

- be hypnotic, helping you stay focused, mindful, and in the present moment,

- provide instant coping strategies to help you safely manage extreme feelings,

- be a combination of words that will summon compassion, composure, forgiveness, and even humor toward children,

- help to reframe most parenting or partnering situations,

- transcend moments of parenting stress, fatigue, and anguish, and

- remind you that you haven't lost your mind.

Science: Reciting positive words or phrases such as "om," "love," and "I am enough" can be powerful, for humans and even for plants. Experiments on plants found they're affected by certain types of sound waves, especially the mantras.

The man-tras and mom-tras have been organized based on topics, from nursing an infant to fitness to eating to dealing with parenting guilt.

Upgrade: Use a mala bead bracelet or necklace to guide your mental reciting of your mantra. Check out the DIY mala bead craft (pages 126-127).

"I Am _____."

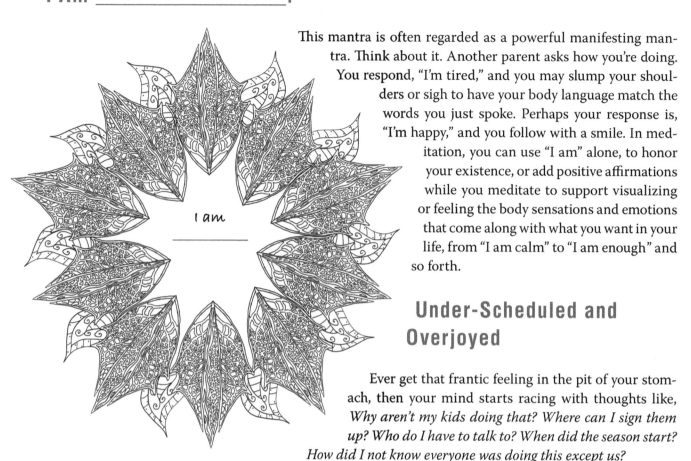

I am
_____

This mantra is often regarded as a powerful manifesting mantra. Think about it. Another parent asks how you're doing. You respond, "I'm tired," and you may slump your shoulders or sigh to have your body language match the words you just spoke. Perhaps your response is, "I'm happy," and you follow with a smile. In meditation, you can use "I am" alone, to honor your existence, or add positive affirmations while you meditate to support visualizing or feeling the body sensations and emotions that come along with what you want in your life, from "I am calm" to "I am enough" and so forth.

Under-Scheduled and Overjoyed

Ever get that frantic feeling in the pit of your stomach, **then** your mind starts racing with thoughts like, *Why aren't my kids doing that? Where can I sign them up? Who do I have to talk to? When did the season start? How did I not know everyone was doing this except us?*

Busyness Is Not a Trophy

When someone asks how you're doing, do you always answer something like, "I'm sooo busy"? In the past, I wore my exhaustion like a trophy, buying into the idea that busyness is a marker of importance, of character, and of economic security. But here's the truth: Busyness is a mark of cognitive overload. This is a state of feeling overwhelmed, which can impair your ability to think creatively, solve problems, make decisions, resist temptations, learn new things easily, remember important social events or information, and regulate your emotions. Practice this mantra to remind you that bragging rights of being busy can have you losing out.

This Won't Matter Tomorrow

This mantra, or the classic "This too shall pass," can be used by parents with children of any age. Perhaps your child breaks something valuable or irreplaceable. Or your toddler spills a full glass of milk across the freshly cleaned floor. Tomorrow's a new day. Floors can be cleaned. Things are things.

Wipe the Slate Clean

After a long, hard day, try the mantra "I wipe the slate clean." Once my kids are asleep in bed, I repeat this in my mind to forgive them for being kids who get on my nerves, throw fits, and talk back. Trust that tomorrow can be better. You can use this mantra in a mindful activity, as well. Just get a small dry erase board or use your child's easel after they go to bed. Write all the things you said or did that you feel parent or partner guilt about. Pause, look at this list, and reflect on it. Then slowly and mindfully erase and let go of all the sources of guilt or other negative feelings, one by one.

Today, I Begin Anew

When you wake up, try practicing the mantra "Today, I begin anew." Nobody has perfected the art of parenting. Be gentle with yourself. Every day is a chance for a new beginning, new lessons, a new take on who we think we are as individuals, parents, and partners. You're not the sum of yesterday's events. With your words and mindful awareness, you can unfold a new day of possibilities in the present.

Inside Me, There's a Quiet Place That Cannot Be Disturbed

We don't often feel like we have alone time as parents. But inside you, you have an inner quiet place that cannot be disturbed. This mantra can be good during particularly rough days.

Soften to the Feeling

When you're feeling any negative feelings, repeating this mantra can help shift your mind-set and soften you. Try doing it with a half-smile on your face (see the "Meditate" section), no matter how hairy and scary the situation.

It's Hard, and Then It's Not

From newborn to toddler to teenage years, your children will go through phases that can feel overwhelming to parent *and* child. They don't last forever. They pass. Struggles with adjusting roles in the home as you welcome your first child pass, as do challenges with breastfeeding, sleep regressions, teething, having a moment in the bathroom, or better yet, in a bath, and yes, even the moments filled with defeat as you try to get a toddler to have more than one bite of a meal. Hard times pass.

Inside me, there's a calm and quiet place that cannot be disturbed

There's Nothing as Soothing as an Exhalation

This mantra reminds us to breathe in trying times.

Curiosity over Comparison

You've likely heard or seen images with the words "Comparison is the thief of joy," a quote by Theodore Roosevelt. While I agree with this, there's no replacement given to parents who find themselves stuck in the comparison trap. These days, we're often comparing our lives, children, and parenting skills to others in baby groups, with colleagues, with neighbors, with family members, and with all our friends on social media. Moving to a place of curiosity over comparison is being more mindful. Curiosity allows us to inquire about the entirety of our experience, from the joyful to the painful. Curiosity can perhaps be understood as an antidote to judgment and other harsh evaluations we may direct toward ourselves or others through the act of comparing. Being curious isn't a natural feeling, but like all other mindfulness practices, it takes, well, practice.

This Feeling Is Temporary

When you're consumed by guilt or anger, say this to remember that your emotions are constantly shifting. There's no need to get locked into a negative feeling that's bound to change. Chances are you'll feel joy and happiness before too long (think: bedtime).

Pause, Then Parent

This really helps ground you when feeling overwhelmed, so you can breathe and then respond to your children rather than react and say something you may regret.

Move Slowly

There's a trend called slow parenting. It's basically mindfulness practices in day-to-day parenting. But its name really resonates with many parents, as we live such fast-paced lives. Do you find yourself constantly telling your kids to "Hurry up" or "Come on, we're late"? A useful activity can be counting how many times a day we're cuing our kids to hurry up. The irony is, we want them to be more patient and not ask us to get a cheese stick out of the fridge twenty times in thirty seconds. If we're more patient and slow down, children and those in our environment pick up the cue.

Breathing in, I Calm My Body; Breathing out, I Smile

This is a quote from the ever-mindfully inspiring Thich Nhat Hanh. When you smile (even in moments when it's the last thing you want to do), you send the message to your brain that you're happy, and it can have an immediate impact on your mood.

There Will Always Be Laundry

We've all had those days: You attack your (or your partner's) to-do list, including loads of laundry; you feel euphoric. The kitchen sink is empty, dishes put away. Then it's bedtime, and you look in the laundry hamper: half-full. There will always be laundry. You look in the sink: dirty bowls and spoons from bedtime snacks. This is something to celebrate; it means you're living. And every sink full of dishes, every load of dirty clothes, towels, sheets, washcloths, and baby blankets represents another day or week that we have lived and been blessed to have a family. So instead of waiting until everything on your to-do list is done to feel balanced, find your balance amidst the dishes and laundry. After all, it's a sign you have food to nourish your family and clothes to dress your family for all your adventures.

There will always be laundry

Lock It In

Mamas and papas, you can also use mantras in positive moments to fill your tank. "Lock it in" can be used in those moments you feel as though your heart could just burst with happiness or pride. Maybe you're sharing a family dinner and your child sweetly says, "This is dee-li-shush," or your kids are teaching each other a new game, or you feel truly appreciated by your partner. Remember that moment. Close your eyes, and lock it in. Then draw from that bank in more challenging parent moments.

Lock it in

I Am a Calm, Confident Leader

This can be a reminder to be calm and confident; it's empowering for parents.

Mindful Parenting and Partnering: Self-Soothing Massage

• • • • • • • • • • • • • • •

Carving out an hour a week for a massage simply isn't realistic for most parents' lives. But you can carve out ten minutes here or two minutes there for a self-soothing massage. This can be anchored to activities you routinely do, such as washing your face, or put in your calendar on a weekly basis. For massage to truly be effective, you must be mindful of your body. Focus your awareness on areas of the body in need of comfort or that assist you in feeling relaxed and soothed. Explore your body and discover what *truly* feels good to you.

Hands

- Apply a dab of lotion or drop of essential oil onto the palm of your hand.
- Rub the palms together.
- Observe heat created by rubbing them together.
- Clasp your hands together, entwining your fingers. Pause for a few seconds.
- Then use your left thumb to massage the area just below your right thumb (palm side) in a circular motion.
- Continue massaging, moving up along the base of each finger.
- Then move inward to the center of the palm.
- Move to your other hand and repeat. Spend approximately two minutes on each hand.

Feet

- This exercise can be done standing or sitting. Use a lacrosse ball, golf ball, or tennis ball. If you're standing, hold the edge of a chair or desk for support.
- Place your right foot on the ball.
- Roll your foot back and forth over the top of the ball.
- Next, place the arch of your foot on top of the ball. Vary pressure.
- Roll the ball around under your arch.
- Roll the ball on the sole of your foot and under your toes and heel.
- Follow the same procedure for your left foot. Spend approximately three to five minutes on each foot.

Eyes

- Briskly rub your palms together, warming your hands.
- Then cup your hands and gently cover your eyes with your palms.
- Keep your eyes covered for approximately one to two minutes.

Ears

- Using your thumbs and index fingers, gently rub your outer ear rims.
- Then rub your ear lobes.
- Do gentle circular motions behind each ear.

Face

- Use the knuckles of your thumbs.
- Gently rub both thumb knuckles up and down along your nose, massaging up and down.
- Then rub circles around your eyes and eyebrows with your fingertips.
- Place your pointer and middle finger near your temples on each side and stroke down your cheekbone gently, dropping off near your chin.
- Place your fingers at your temple again and repeat.

Head

- Sit down in a chair or stool and rest your elbows on a desk or table.
- Place your fingertips on your scalp beneath your hair.
- Massage your head with your fingertips, starting from your hair line and working toward the top of your head.
- You can use essential oil if you like, but always consult a health care professional before using essential oils.

Science: Massage can improve blood circulation, reduce muscle tension, improve sleep, and increase relaxation. If you and your partner want to massage each other, research has found this benefits both partners' well-being, regardless of who is giving or receiving (Naruse, Cornellissen, and Moss 2018).

Explore: The emphasis here is on self-care for mamas and papas, but know that you can use these techniques for your littles as part of the winding-down routine for bedtime. Check out the Mindful Bedtime Routine for Minis on page 32 that includes massage techniques for parents to use with kids.

Mindful Parenting and Partnering: Mindful Mama and Papa Moments

• • • • • • • • • • • • •

While I've trained in mindfulness and teach it to my clients, I too am a mama and often find it difficult to find time to practice. Sometimes, I need reminding. Don't beat yourself up about this. Or perhaps in this moment, it feels overwhelming to flip through this book to try a longer activity. That's okay. You can try a quick activity, like the ones I've dubbed Mindful Mama and Papa Moments, found here.

Here are exercises that will help you practice being mindful in your life as busy mamas and papas. Because when we practice mindfulness, we're *exercising* our attention muscle, becoming *mentally fitter*.

Five Things

- Pause for a moment.
- Take five deep belly breaths following each inhale and exhale fully through.
- Look around you and notice five things you see.
- Next notice five things you hear.
- Next notice five things you feel in contact with your body (such as the air on your face, your feet on the floor, and so on).
- Take another five deep belly breaths.
- Carry this awareness and openness onto the next moments of your day.

Mindful Daily Interaction

Parents, choose one routine interaction you have with your child daily—breast feeding, brushing teeth, walking to school, bedtime routine—and set an intention to be fully present in this interaction for a particular time frame (e.g., five days a week for two weeks). Reflect on this experience after that time frame is up. Questions to reflect on include "What did I notice about where my mind goes when I'm not as present with my children?" and "What possibilities has this mindful daily interaction practice created for my relationship with my child?"

Mindful Cleaning

There'll always be laundry and other household chores. You can find joy in the mundane and make household chores exercises in mindfulness. (I know, I know, but instead of rolling your eyes, roll up your sleeves and give this a try.) When cleaning, do it as if you were washing your baby in their first bath in the days following birth. Take the time to be fully aware of each surface, crevice, or dish you are washing, being fully aware of the movement of your hands, the cloth or brush or vacuum you hold, the scents in the air, the signs of space, dishes, and clothes well lived in. Do not be dragged into the future by thinking about what task you'll do next. Be in the present moment of cleaning, having gratitude for the moment and the material you have in your life to clean, from dishes to floors and, yes, even toilets.

Mindful Shower

In our house, Jon's morning shower is his first mindful moment, setting the tone for the day. You too can benefit from setting a mindful tone for the day, lowering your stress levels and awakening the senses for the day ahead. How can you sprinkle your shower with mindful awareness for a mindful moment? Try one or all of these tips and tools:

- **Breathe.** When you first step into the shower, take one deep inhale through the nose to the count of 4, hold for 7, and take an extended exhale through the mouth to a count of 8. Sigh as you exhale. Do a few cycles of this breathing exercise to start your shower time. This is your moment, here and now; you have nowhere else to be.

- **Smell.** Use toxin-free body wash, soap bars, and essential oils to engage your senses. You can also put a couple drops of essential oil on the floor of the shower. Close your eyes and inhale the aroma deeply.

- **Feel.** Notice the glide of the soap bar or the gritty exfoliating effect of soap suds or a loofah along your skin. Notice the temperature of the water and how it varies head to toe. Notice the texture of your hair between your fingers as you wash it.

- **Listen.** There are layers of sound in the shower: the sound of the water coming from the shower head, the sound of lathering shampoo in your hair, the sound of treating your skin with a scrub.

- **See.** Watch the bubbles forming on your skin; notice the water cascading down your body and swirling down the shower drain.

- **Mind the mind.** It's easy to think of a million things in the shower, from the emails waiting in your inbox to what to make for breakfast, using those minutes you're in the shower to plan your day. The mind will naturally wander in the shower; it takes practice and anchoring into your senses with the tips above to start to be more mindful in the sensual experience of a shower.

Mindful Parenting and Partnering: The Mindful Bedtime Routine for Children

• • • • • • • • • • • • •

Science: Researchers have found a bedtime routine embodies the characteristics of nurturing care and early childhood stimulation. It has been described as a cost-effective method of promoting positive childhood development (Mindell and Williamson 2017).

I've never liked how some parents of young kids call the hours between 6 and 8 p.m. the "witching hours." I don't know about you, but if I ascribe those words to a couple hours a day it strips them of any possibility of joy. Of course, bedtime isn't always easy, smooth, or full of giggles. But you can infuse mindfulness and a degree of structure to provide children with a sense of certainty and security, and practice emotional and behavioral regulation.

Child development specialists and researchers have identified building blocks of a bedtime routine for young children, including the following:

- nutrition (e.g., feeding, healthy snack)
- hygiene (e.g., bathing and teeth cleaning)
- communication (e.g., reading, singing lullabies)
- physical contact (e.g., massage, cuddling, rocking)

Many of these components are included here. You can bring these exercises and tools into the bedtime routine so you wrap it up feeling fulfilled, rather than utterly drained. From using essential oils for a bedtime massage to breathing exercises with your child's favorite stuffed animal: whatever you choose, practice it regularly as part of your bedtime routine.

Mindful of the Need for Zzzs

Sleep hygiene is so important, no matter what age you are. Both the brain and the body need sleep. While we sleep, we consolidate what we learned throughout the day. When children don't rest long enough, they may feel tired or cranky, have a hard time following directions, or be unable to think clearly the next day.

When establishing a daily structure, sleep plays a prominent role. You want your children to wake up and go to sleep at approximately the same time every day. Sleep can determine what your child's day looks like.

Develop an end-of-day routine for your child. Engaging in the same activities at the end of the day signals to their brain (just like it does for adults) that the day is coming to an end, and it's time for bed. Examples include taking a bath, brushing your teeth, reading a bedtime story, having a cup of milk or water, and meditating. Some families find it helpful to have a visual chart in the bathroom for kids to see, with the time at the top that bedtime routine starts, and the time at the end where the bedtime routine should be drawn to a close, and visual depictions of tasks to do during the routine (a picture of a bath, a toothbrush, a book).

Counting Breaths over Sheep

For children, the activity of counting their breaths can help calm their nervous system and assist with relaxing before bed. This is an activity that parents can do together with their children. Here's how:

- Close your eyes.
- Find stillness.
- Focus on your breathing, not necessarily changing it in any way.
- Pay attention to your breathing.
- Count your breaths. Inhale 1. Exhale 2. Inhale 3. Exhale 4. (And so forth, until relaxed; you'll be able to tell if your child has relaxed.)
- If your attention wanders, simply return to your breath and repeat the sequence.

Bedtime Breathing Buddy

Your child can involve her or his favorite stuffie in a bedtime mindfulness of breathing activity to help bring on rest and relaxation, for parents and children. This exercise is on page 56.

Essential Bedtime Oils

Make bedtime "scent-tual." Here are some oils and essential oil blends you may want to try (always refer to a health care practitioner when using oils with children or pregnant/nursing mothers):

- lavender
- lavender and orange
- bergamot and lavender and patchouli and ylang-ylang
- frankincense and lavender
- or choose your and your child's favorite blend from the essential crafting blends on page 115.

Mindful Mini Massage

Massages aren't just for mamas and papas. Massage is not only soothing for your child, but it's also a way to emotionally and physically connect with one another.

- **Start young.** Start around age six months and up.
- **Soft touch.** As you introduce massage, have a light pressure (but not *too* light or your child will become ticklish).
- **See your child.** Pay attention during the massage time to your child's body language while you're massage him or her. You'll be able to gauge what they do and do not enjoy. Use slow, open-handed strokes or circular motions.
- **Arm or leg massage.** Use open-handed strokes while massaging toward the heart. When on limbs, start at the hand/foot or wrist/ankle and move slowly toward the elbow/knee, and so forth.
- **Hand or foot massage.** Have your child lie down in bed in a relaxed position. If they have been exposed to yoga, you can instruct them to find savasana, or resting pose. With a bit of oil or lotion on your hands, use a circular motion, starting at the bottom base of the big toe or thumb. Massage the

base of each finger/toe with this circular motion. Work your way along each finger/toe in sequence, squeezing gently to provide stimulation.

Science: Research has shown that massage can ease anxiety, reduce pain, and speed healing in children. Nurturing touch has also been shown to help children with social, motor, and cognitive development as well as emotional regulation.

Mindful Partnering and Parenting:
The Mindful Bedtime Routine for Teens and Parents

• • • • • • • • • • • • • • • •

Bedtime routines aren't just for kids; they're essential for teens and parents too. Try these tips for a mindful and nourishing evening routine. Make your nighttime routine a habit using the reward system on pages 37-38.

Set a Tech Bedtime

Set a time to shut down those activities that stimulate your mind, such as work, email, internet browsing, and even watching TV. The general guideline is to try to avoid backlit devices at night because these screens are stimulating to the eyes and brain, sending the message that it's daytime and therefore awake time. Try reading a book, taking a bath with bath salts or oils, listening to music, or practicing some gentle yoga or meditation.

Brain Dump

Dump it all out. Write lists, or jot down all of the things you're stressing about. Try not to do this right before bed, but rather before your "power-down" time to help your mind let these worries go.

Eat, Drink, and Move Mindfully

Caffeine isn't bad, but it is a stimulant and should be used mindfully. If you're experiencing sleeping problems, cutting back on caffeine may help. It's also a good idea to avoid eating a particularly heavy meal late in the evening; you want to go to bed satiated but not overly full. Some medications and supplements can also affect sleep, so it's best to get educated about what you're taking. Remember that exercise is one of your best friends when it comes to managing overall stress levels. However, intense exercise late at night isn't recommended for anyone experiencing sleeping problems. It may be better to do your high-intensity training during the daytime, leaving the evenings for yoga or stillness. Looking for a drink to include in your nighttime routine? Check out the Night-Turm Latte (on page 165).

Meditate

Start by lying on the floor or sitting on a yoga mat, bed, couch, chair, or meditation cushion. Feel grounding with and support at any points of contact between your body and the surface below you. Close your eyes. Remind yourself you have nowhere else to be. This moment is a gift. Inhale deeply through your nose, and exhale through your mouth. Notice the gap at the end of each breath. This shifts us from the sympathetic (fight-or-flight) to our parasympathetic (rest and digest) nervous system. Bring awareness to your breath for ten minutes. If your mind wanders—and it will—gather your awareness with your next inhale, without judgment or criticism for having a monkey mind. If you're looking for tools to support your meditation practice, you can check out Insight Timer, a free app that has a meditation timer and thousands of guided meditations. Another app is Calm, which has sleep stories and music to support sleep.

Mindful Parenting and Partnering: Reward Systems for Minis

• • • • • • • • • • • • • •

Routines are helpful in shaping behavior, and building reward systems and token economies can be supportive for kids' health and development at home, at school, and in the community. Here is a complete outline of how to mindfully build a reward system.

This reward system is based on the psychology practice of the token economy: a system of behavior modification based on the systematic reinforcement of a target behavior. The reinforcers are symbols or tokens that can be exchanged for other reinforcers (or rewards). A token is an object or symbol that can be exchanged for material reinforcers, services, or privileges.

Tokens

A variety of tokens can be used: stickers, coins, checkmarks. These symbols are comparably worthless outside of the caregiver-child relationship, but their value lies in the fact they can be exchanged for other things.

Reinforcers

A variety of reinforcers can also be used:

- **material reinforcers:** Books, money, preferred food (try to keep nutritious so as not to create a "junk food as reward" mentality)
- **services**: Baking healthy muffins with mom or dad or grandparents, having room cleaned for child, going to the zoo or science center
- **privileges:** extra screen time on computer or tablet, permission to read an extra book at bedtime, calling a grandparent or family member or friend, having your name or picture on the wall

Target Behaviors

There is a large range of possible target behaviors, including self-care, attending activities, academic behavior, disruptive behavior, sibling relations. A token economy is more than just using exchangeable tokens. For a token economy to work, criteria have to be clearly specified. For example, if the target behavior is doing a bedtime routine, the time frame to be completed in as well as all tasks (taking a bath, brushing teeth, reading a book, meditation, lights out) need to be clearly outlined for the child.

Optional Punishment by Loss of Tokens

Some systems include the possibility of punishment by token loss. For example, disruptive behavior or temper tantrum in the grocery store can be fined with the loss of tokens. This response cost should be clearly specified for children before the token economy system is set in place. If children are mature enough, they can be involved in specifying these contingencies.

Mindful Parenting and Partnering:
Reward Systems for Mamas and Papas

• • • • • • • • • • • • • •

We often hear of reward systems for kids. But adults thrive when praised and rewarded too. Thus, reward systems can be supportive during the stage when working on developing new habits. Like, oh, I don't know; a mindful routine, perhaps? Just think of local yoga studios offering thirty-day yoga challenges to support members in building the habit of yoga. Participants are awarded a star sticker for each yoga class completed.

Self-Care Routines Are Worth Rewarding

Self-care isn't selfish, but many parents only emphasize self-care for their kids (proper sleep, bathing, glass of milk to transition to bedtime, and so on). It's time to rid yourself of guilt and realize your mind, body, and family will benefit from shifting activities from your daily "self-care-that's-never-gonna-happen wish list" to your daily ritual. Think simple acts, from soaking in the tub with essential oils and Epsom salts for ten minutes, using hand lotion to self-massage your hands or feet, engaging in a shared breathing exercise with your partner to attune to each other's state in a given moment, or making time for a daily meditation practice.

Tokens

A variety of tokens can be used for adults as with kids: stickers or checkmarks on a chart or journal. Crafting stores now have DIY agendas, and you can usually find an array of stickers to choose.

Reinforcers

A variety of reinforcers can be used:

- **Material reinforcers:** Books, money, a self-development course or retreat, preferred food.
- **Services**: Having a partner take on a chore that's typically yours for a day/week/month, or hiring someone to assist with a deep clean.
- **Privileges and other extras:** You can get creative with this one.

Target Behaviors

There is a large range of possible target behaviors, including self-care attending activities, and family communication. A token economy is more than just using exchangeable tokens. For a token economy to work, criteria have to be specified and clear. For example, if the target behavior is for mom to build a thirty-minute yoga practice into her day, the time frame to be completed in as well as all tasks (e.g., set alarm thirty minutes earlier than usual before family awakens, choose an online yoga class to guide, lay out yoga mat in designated space) need to be clearly outlined for the family in order to create expectations and boundaries for the family and self to respect and attend to in this habit-building phase.

Optional Punishment by Loss of Tokens

As with your children, the possibility of punishment by token loss is included in your reward system. For example, yelling at your children or breaking technology use rules can be fined with the loss of tokens. This response cost should be clearly specified when developing the token economy system.

> **Science**: The intrinsic value of self-care for parents spans from boosted mental clarity, stress reduction, and boosted productivity at work and home. The extrinsic benefits include role modeling the importance and commonality parents and kids both have on the self-care train.

Mindful Parenting and Partnering: Gratitude

• • • • • • • • • • • • • • • •

You cannot discuss mindfulness without highlighting gratitude. We hear a lot about the importance of being grateful for fleeting moments with our children or about starting a dedicated gratitude journal practice. But let's cover the basics about what, how, and why to practice gratitude.

Gratitude Defined

The word *gratitude* is derived from the Latin word *gratia*, which means grace, graciousness, or gratefulness. Gratitude is a thankful appreciation for what an individual receives, whether tangible or intangible. We acknowledge the goodness in our lives, which often involves recognizing that the source of that goodness lies at least partially outside ourselves. Gratitude connects all ages to something larger than ourselves.

Why Practice Gratitude?

Over the years, studies have linked gratitude to greater life satisfaction, increased social support, and decreased rates of stress and depression. Gratitude helps people feel more positive emotions, relish good experiences, improve their health, deal with adversity, and build strong relationships. Gratitude can have such a powerful impact on your life because it engages your brain in a virtuous cycle. Your brain only has so much power to focus its attention. It cannot easily focus on both positive and negative stimuli. It's not always easy to remember to be grateful, particularly since the human brain is so adaptable. Gratitude takes practice, like any other skill.

How to Practice Gratitude

- **Start a gratitude journal.** Check out the Mindful Journalling activity on pages 134-135 for tips on starting a journaling practice, including gratitude journaling. It can be a journal dedicated to gratitude practice or five bullets of gratitude in one's agenda daily.
- **Write a thank-you note.** You can make yourself happier and nurture your relationship with another person—family member or otherwise—by writing a thank-you letter expressing your appreciation of that person's impact on your life. Deliver the hand-written note under a bedroom door, by mail, or in person. Aim for crafting one gratitude letter a month.
- **Thank someone mentally.** If you don't have time to journal or write a note, it may help just to think about someone who has done something nice for you and mentally thank the individual.
- **Meditate on gratitude.** Mindfulness meditation involves the practice of focused awareness in the present moment. Try to focus on what you're grateful for (the warmth of the sun, a healthy baby, a pleasant scent).

Science: A study from the National Institutes of Health examined blood flow in the brain while subjects summoned up feelings of gratitude (Zahn et al. 2009). Feelings of gratitude directly activated brain regions associated with the neurotransmitter dopamine. Dopamine feels good to get, which is why it's considered the reward neurotransmitter. But dopamine is also important in initiating action.

Mindful Parenting and Partnering: Mindful Family Stress and Conflict Busters

• • • • • • • • • • • • • • •

Life is stressful. It's hard to always feel zen when you have a number of commitments (adults and kids alike) and gadgets constantly vying for your attention.

Ever lash out on your partner, only to be filled instantly with regret? The times we get in trouble with our partners are, more often than not, when we're tuned out, distracted, or not paying attention to what's really happening in the moment; instead, we're reliving a past hurt or fantasizing about a future crisis. The internal and external awareness that comes with mindfulness practice will help you avoid emotional land mines and support you in getting off autopilot and into the driver's seat of your life now. This is not to say you will never have a spat with your partner. Rather, mindful awareness to you and your partner's needs and communication styles can teach you how to fight fair in a less reactive state.

Here are some stress and conflict busters you can try out:

Take a Break (the *New* Time-Out)

The name "time-outs" has a negative connotation. So in the practice on mindfulness, families can try reframing "time-outs" as "taking a break" or "hitting pause." We all need breaks sometimes, parents and kids alike. Sometimes as parents, we'll have to instruct our child to take a break, but we may even have to encourage ourselves or our partners at times to take a break.

Two methods you can try for taking a break:

1) **Designate a chair in the house as the "quiet chair."** This is a place where you can retreat to decelerate conflicts. Have boundaries around the chair, such that if you see someone in the chair, you don't talk to them but rather give them space and leave them to have some silence, collect their thoughts, and regulate their emotions.

2) **Walk around the block.** Walk mindfully, feeling the pressure in your feet as each foot hits the ground, heel to toe. Visualize yourself "stamping out" the fire in your head or your body. Obviously, you won't send small children out for a walk around the block on their own. You can guide them on the walk, encouraging them to visualize stamping out the fire, or have them walk in the backyard or inside in an open area, where you supervise them while also giving some space.

Be the First to Apologize

This is a way to restore household harmony. It's not always easy. But it's a good practice to help parents move past conflict. It also sets a good example for children.

Build a Mindful Routine

From my personal and professional experience, children and teens are experience some of the same stress-related problems their parents do. Take the guesswork and some of the stress out of the daily activities of wake times, mealtimes, and bedtimes. Let everyone in the family relax into the predictable flow of a healthy and secure life.

Reduce Screen Time

Mindfulness and the act of being present doesn't jibe well with constantly being connected with technological devices or TV screens when in the presence of loved ones. By disconnecting, we're being mindful of the needs of self-care and family connection. The benefits are plentiful: less comparison of one's life to another's highlight reel on social media, more eye contact to support communication among family members, and simply more time to follow other passions or complete some tasks. This isn't to say Netflix binging is bad or you should judge yourself in parenting or partnering if you or your children have a screen in front of them. Just be mindful of your use and how it may impact conflicts or communication in the home.

> **Explore**: Looking to learn more about technoference? Check out pages 45-46. If you want to take action and put pen to paper to build a customized Tech Use Contract with your family, flip to pages 47-49.

Mindful Parenting and Partnering:
Five Ways Families Can Slow Down

• • • • • • • • • • • • •

Remember all the time you had when you were a child, aimlessly wandering, exploring, being curious about the world around you? Do you still have that time and space? Do your children? When someone asks how you are, you may always say, "Busy." Many families feel overwhelmed, moving at a frantic pace, working and juggling childcare, fitness classes, organized sports, multiple play dates, constant bombardment of notifications from our smart phones. We can choose to slow down and simplify our schedules. Make time for mindfulness practice, which has been shown to reduce stress and cluttered minds that come from the frantic pace we often run at. Here are five tips for slowing down your family, now:

1. Play Time Prevails

A playful attitude brings lightness, curiosity, and joy to any situation. Parents and kids deserve and need time for play. So add it to your to-do list today. This may mean choosing just one structured activity or class outside of childcare/school for your child. In turn, this reduces the time you as parents serve as taxi drivers and enhances the time you can be playing too.

2. Block Email Checking

I challenge you to check email just two or three times a day. For example, set a time after meals or snacks, if those are on regular intervals. Turn off notifications that may interrupt you outside of your chosen blocks. This is for a day at work or a day with kids. You're likely to get more done and be more focused.

3. Do One Thing at a Time

Practice mindfulness of the present moment. Notice when you are in the past or the future, then label it without judgment: "remembering" or "thinking." And then come back to whatever it is you're doing. When playing, play. When walking, walk. When being intimate, be intimate. When eating, eat.

4. Make Time for the Busy and the Calm Days

Most families, my own included, like to have some big, fun, exciting days. Likewise, at times, we're under-scheduled and overjoyed with that, as well. No matter what our age, we all crave downtime to relax, process, and refresh. Experiencing one allows us to appreciate the other.

5. Just Say No

If saying yes to a friend, colleague, a group you volunteer with, or an acquaintance in the neighborhood means adding too much to your day, or if you really just don't want to be there, then say no and don't go. And then let go of the guilt and shoulds, and move on with your full life, fully showing up to what you say yes to.

Mindful Parenting and Partnering:
Seven Tips for Mindful Communication

• • • • • • • • • • • • •

Parenting stresses, work pressures, and oppressive inner dialogues can all contribute to adult stress. And who do we often take it out on? Those closest to us. If you're in a relationship, it can be your loved one. Mindfulness can help us communicate more clearly, effectively, and meaningfully. By talking to your partner mindfully, with your full attention, you create connection and real opportunities for engagement.

How can parents bring more awareness and responsiveness and less reactivity to communication with one another? This list is compiled from a host of experts in mindfulness, relationships, and communication, including Susan Chapman, Thich Nhat Hanh, and John Gottman. Try any and all of these practices to bring more mindfulness to the communication patterns between you and your partner.

1. Listen with Intention and Attention

Ever find yourself listening so you have the wittiest, snarkiest, or quickest reply? It's common to listen with the intention of replying rather than understanding. This involves summoning the intention to have a genuine interest in your partner's views, experiences, needs, and emotions, along with the attention required to stay present and open to receive your partner's words, no matter what they are. You can practice this with a structured mindful communication exercise. One partner listens, intently, to the other's voice and words; the other simply speaks and ends with a simple acknowledgment, like "Thank you." The partner who has the floor can share whatever he or she chooses. Then switch roles.

2. Use "I" Statements

Instead of saying, "You always …," "You are being too …," and other less-than-constructive communication lines that are common in parent relationships, use "I" statements. Acknowledge your feelings, thoughts, and body sensations in the present moment and the state you're seeking for mind-body-heart.

3. Pause to Notice Patterns

We all have automatic responses that shape how we respond to others, *especially* our partners. Like going down a dirt road again and again, we get stuck in those ruts in the road, and it takes mindful awareness to pause and notice the communication patterns we have with our partners. By noticing patterns shaped by past experiences or conditions, we can break patterns that lead to arguments.

4. Practice Nonjudgment

To mindfully converse and avoid conflict with your partner, try your best to refrain from judging your partner's opinion, story, or perspective. There's no wrong or right, only different perceptions.

5. Be Compassionate and Do No Harm

Hurtful speech toward our partners is not necessary. Buddhists believe that harmful words that come out of our mouths are a double-edged sword; they will hurt us as much as they will hurt others.

6. Continually Show Interest in Learning about Each Other

The honeymoon phase is over in your relationship, but that doesn't mean your interest in each other's passions and inner workings should wane with it. Take the time to ask your partner questions. Even if you've been married decades, there are still things you don't know about each other. Ask his or her thoughts, feelings, memories, future goals, activities they are interested in trying for the first time, and more.

7. Express Gratitude

Regularly thank your partner for something specific she or he does that makes your life better in some way, big or small. Even the mundane, such as picking up your favorite yogurt while getting groceries, is worthy of acknowledgment.

I am grateful for

_____

Mindful Parenting and Partnering: Technoference

• • • • • • • • • • • • • •

Technology use is a hot topic in my practice and my home. Mamas and papas, this topic extends from your relationship with each other as parents, to your relationship with your children, as well as with each family member's social circle. Let's dive into the science of how tech use, social media likes, and posting can be addictive and habit forming; mindfulness can be used to reduce the negative impact of technology and mitigate its impact on our most cherished relationships.

Science: Technoference is a growing area of research. Researchers have been examining how constant texting leads people to pay attention to their cell phones instead of communicating with their partner. This can lead to conflicts between partners due to texting behavior and lack of intimacy stemming from texting activities that displace focus on the romantic partner (Halpern and Katz 2017). Heavy parent tech use has been associated with suboptimal parent-child interactions, as well as problem behaviors among children (McDaniel and Radesky 2018).

Upgrade: Try making a DIY basket for cell phones for the family or for when guests come for dinner. Example found on page 143.

Reducing Technoference

Here are some ways to reduce technoference:

- **Ask yourself if you have a techno-addiction.** After you become more mindful of the issue, you can better assess to what extent screen usage is actually disruptive to your interactions with family in the precious time you have together. This can also be an honest conversation with your partner or children. Children are naturally mindful and will often give you honest answers about how they perceive your use of technology. Then reverse the tables and talk to them about their technology use. In order to raise children who use technology respectfully and responsibly, you as a parent should look at your own technology use and ensure you're modeling respectful and responsible behavior.

- **Make tech-free zones.** Agree with your partner and children on places (like the bedroom) and times (definitely recommend during mealtimes) when everyone puts their phones or tablets out of reach and on silent in order to spend technology-free time together. Include TV in this discussion as well, talking about where and when the television can be viewed.

- **Know there'll be hurdles, and prepare for them.** You're human. Things come up (like a forgotten invoice a client needs by end of day, etc.). Make a plan for how best you as parents can deal with those hurdles while not disrupting the moment with your family. Make a sticky note or jot on your to-do list for yourself to do it later.

- **Make a Family Tech Contract.** Sit down together and draft up a contract that clearly states tech-free areas in the home, tech use, tech-free time frames, when cell phones and tablets go to bed at night, and more. Use the template provided here. You can personalize it and put it up somewhere everyone in the home can see it. In creating this contract with your children that attends to your concerns regarding their use of technology, you must also address what your children expect of your use of technology. Many children and teens express frustrations with parents who check their cell phones for texts during dinner or when watching their child perform.

- **Have rewards and consequences for breaking tech use contract terms.** Some families find it supportive to have consequences for breaking terms of the contract (e.g., putting a loonie in a technojar, funds for which go toward a shared family activity like family yoga class). This solidifies expectations and allows parents and children alike to take seriously not only the responsibilities you have today but also those that will emerge in life. Parents, emphasize you will always be available for guidance and direction in relation to your child's or teen's use of technology.

Family Tech Use Contract

The following family members (first and last names): _____
_____
agree to the undersigned contract for technology use both inside and outside the home, effective
(date): _____. We all understand that part of a parent's job is to guide
technology use, and that it's a family's responsibility to keep open and honest communication
about technology use.

Tech Use Space and Time

The following areas of the home are designated tech-free zones:
_____
_____

Each evening, our family's phones and tablets go to bed promptly at: _____
in the following location: _____.
Phone wake-up time is _____ for adults _____ for children.

The children in our home can use cell phones or tablets during the following time frames/activities on weekdays:
_____
_____

The adults in our home can use cell phones or tablets or laptops during the following time frames/activities on weekdays:
_____
_____

The children in our home can use cell phones or tablets during the following time frames/activities on weekends:

_____

_____

The adults in our home can use cell phones or tablets or laptops during the following time frames/activities on weekends:

_____

_____

Opportunities to earn extra _____ minutes of screen time:

I will keep my head up when walking indoors and outdoors, not looking down at my phone, so I can witness and appreciate the world and beings around me instead of on my screen.

I will not check my phone during family meals or during these agreed-upon family time (e.g., movies, activities on vacation): _____.

I will turn off or silence my phone when in public at restaurants, at the movies, or when speaking with others.

The adults in the home will devote ten minutes weekly to sitting with each child in the home to give their full attention and learn about what each child finds fun to play or watch online. This technology show-and-tell will take place the following day and time frame weekly:

_____

Safety and Sensibility

The adults in the home will always know the passwords for each child's technology device. Other ways adults will monitor phone include _____.

I will not use my technological devices to lie, embarrass, tease, deceive, or bully another person (family, friend, strangers). This can include but is not limited to using my words, spreading rumors, or sharing photos/videos. I will not involve myself in conversations that are hurtful to others. I will not send a message to anyone that I would not say in person.

I will never send inappropriate pictures to anyone from my phone or tablet.

I will tell my parents if someone online makes me feel unsafe, sad, fearful, or uncomfortable.

I will not share any private information (full name, birthday, address) online without permission of my parents.

Consequences for Breaking Terms of Contract

I understand I risk the following consequences if I break any of the above terms (specific adult and child consequences):

1. _____
2. _____
3. _____
4. _____

Signed By:

_____   _____   _____

_____   _____   _____

(Above signed by all children in home)

_____   _____

(Signed by all parents/caregivers in home)

In this chapter, you've learned ways to bring mindful awareness to what are otherwise quite routine parenting activities that you do on autopilot daily: showering, washing the dishes, morning coffee, and so on. Before you go to bed each night, reflect on one routine activity that you brought mindful awareness to during the day.

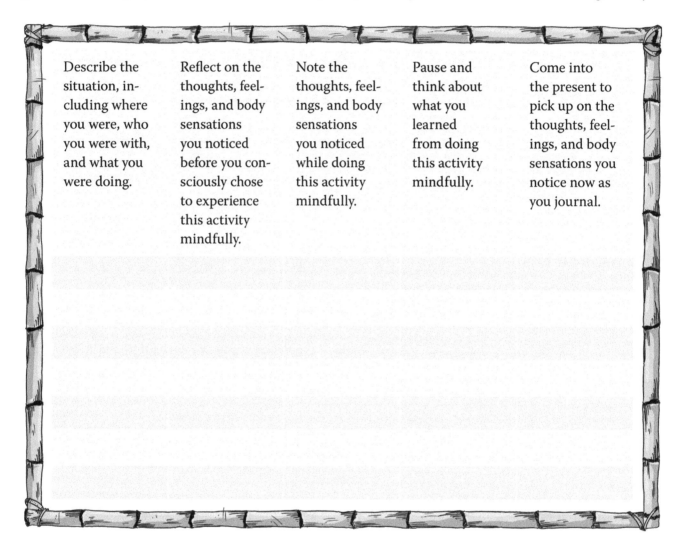

Describe the situation, including where you were, who you were with, and what you were doing.	Reflect on the thoughts, feelings, and body sensations you noticed before you consciously chose to experience this activity mindfully.	Note the thoughts, feelings, and body sensations you noticed while doing this activity mindfully.	Pause and think about what you learned from doing this activity mindfully.	Come into the present to pick up on the thoughts, feelings, and body sensations you notice now as you journal.

Breathe

· · · · · · · · · · · · · ·

Breathe: Introduction

· · · · · · · · · · · · · ·

In birthing classes, in yoga classes, and of course in the birthing process, breath work is an activity that parents-to-be are hyper focused on. Moms taking the deepest breaths of their lives. Grandparents, moms, or dads coaching their child or partner in deep breathing and relaxation. And yet somehow, when we get our children in our arms and become parents, we hold our breath, sometimes feeling like we're drowning. A few deep breaths, the practice of awareness of breath, can be what saves a mama and papa in those overwhelming moments.

Just Breathe

The breath is always with you as a refocusing tool to bring you back to the present moment. Your breath is an anchor you can return to over and over again when you become distracted by thoughts, plans, problems, emotions, or physical discomfort.

Deep breathing or belly breathing is technically called diaphragmatic breathing. It involves the lungs expanding downward, pressing on the diaphragmatic wall, allowing much more air to be inhaled than with chest breathing. The diaphragmatic wall in turn pushes on the abdominal cavity. The abdominal cavity expands and presses on the spine and the vagus nerve, a cranial nerve that runs down the spine from the brain stem. The vagus nerve turns on the body's relaxation system and regulates the parasympathetic nervous system when pressed on in this way. This way of breathing also activates the prefrontal cortex of the brain (the thinking part of the brain). So next time someone tells you to take a deep breath, reflect on this and perhaps share this science lesson.

Science: Breathing patterns impact humans on a conscious and unconscious level. For example, newborns in same room as their mama for a period after birth regulate breathing more readily and have lower instance of SIDS than babies who do not sleep in same room as mama. Taking deep breaths has the ability to shift us from the stressed sympathetic nervous system to our rest-and-digest parasympathetic nervous system.

Breathe: Belly Breathing Basics

• • • • • • • • • • • • • • • •

The breath is the simplest tool we have for mindful awareness. Attending to our breath is a simple, practical, and effective way to boost mindful awareness for all ages, anytime, anywhere. You'll learn an array of breathing exercises in this book, from on the mat to your first cup of coffee in the morning. But for now, let's strip it back to the basics. Being mindful of breath is a proven technique for practicing mindfulness.

Age Range: 2+

Directions

- **Breathing basics for one and all.** This is an exercise you can do solo, one-on-one with a child, or as a whole family.

- **Place the hands.** Put one hand on your belly, the other on your chest. Breathe naturally. Notice which hand moves more. Hint: you want it to be the one on your belly.

- **Inhale.** Take a breath in through the nose to a count of 4. Feel the belly under your hand completely filling with air.

- **Exhale.** Blow out gently through your mouth to the count of 8, just like you are blowing a huge bubble. Feel the belly deflate under your hand.

- **Repeat.** There is no set number of times to repeat, but aim for three or four while gauging the age and experiences of participants.

- **Reflect on and get curious about the act of breathing.** Ask questions below as you feel fit:

  - How did you learn to breathe?
  - What do you notice when you breathe quickly?
  - What do you notice when you breathe slowly?
  - When you exhaled long and slow, did you run out of air or have some left over?
  - Where and when can you see yourself using deep breathing exercises?

Upgrade: If you find you or your child is predominantly a chest or shallow breather, try sitting or standing up with a straight back and clasping the hands behind the back. Relax the abdominal muscles so your stomach can move out as your lungs press on your stomach. Notice the movement that easily comes to the belly as you breathe. You can also try clasping your hands behind your head to open the chest area and make taking deeper breaths easier.

Breathe: A Family Breathing Exercise to Start the Day

• • • • • • • • • • • • • • •

It's not always possible to have a smooth morning, between prepping lunches, filling backpacks, arranging diaper bags, making coffee, feeding the dog, cleaning oatmeal that's been tossed across the kitchen: You name it. Parents, you have a lot going on in the morning, even if you've gone to bed the night before feeling fully prepared for the busy day ahead. To avoid starting your day in a frenzy, try the following ritual of sharing a morning breath with your partner or children.

Age Range: All ages

Directions

- Stop in your tracks before breakfast to find your grounding. Simply pause in your bedroom with your partner, or stand with your children in their room or the hallway outside their room where you meet for the morning.

- Hold hands.

- Close your eyes or look down toward clasped hands.

- Take three deep inhales and exhales in sync. Mindfully tune into your partner or child's breath to get a sense of what they are experiencing in the moment.

- Move along to a nourishing breakfast in a state that supports rest and digestion.

- Take on the day.

Upgrade: If getting young children dressed in the morning is a particularly hairy situation in your home, try this exercise right before dressing in your child's bedroom.

Breathe: Mandala Colouring Page

· · · · · · · · · · · ·

"Each morning
we are born again.
What we do today is
what matters most."

—Buddha

Breathe: Mindful Mini's Belly Breathing Buddy Exercise

• • • • • • • • • • • • • • • •

In our household, the kids are rockin' through their activities, school, play, all day. Yet rolling quietly into bed at the end of the day doesn't come naturally to them. To get things moving, we find this breathing exercise helpful. Use to prep for nap time or bedtime, or to soothe an upset child.

Age Range: 2–8

Materials

• Stuffed animal
• Surface to lie down on (bare floor, yoga mat, bed, couch)

Directions

• Have your child pick a stuffed animal and find a comfortable spot to lie down on the floor or bed.

• Put on calming music (or nature sounds, if preferred).

• Encourage your child to close her or his eyes (if comfortable), and allow the arms to rest naturally at the side, with legs flopped out from the body.

• Guide your child to relax and feel all his or her weight dropping down onto the floor or bed.

• Place the stuffed animal on your child's tummy.

• Encourage your child to take deep breaths, rocking the stuffed animal to sleep with the motion of his or her tummy going up and down with each inhale and exhale.

    • You can say, "You're safe, and all you have to do right now is breathe. Can you feel the weight of the stuffed animal on your tummy? Imagine your stuffie is riding the wave of your breath. As you inhale, you're fillllllllling your tummy with air, and stuffie is rocking alllll the way up to the sky. And when you breathe out, your tummy empties and stuffie is falling back down toward the ground. What a ride! Stuffie finds it very soothing. It's stuffie's bedtime. So just keep breathing normally, rocking your stuffie to sleep with your deep, gentle, and steady breaths."

Upgrade: This is a great exercise for families to use when traveling and staying outside the comfort of your child's home and bed. You child can also try this activity while lying down listening to music.

Science: In a study by Flook et al. (2015), there was an activity called "belly buddies" in which kids listened to music while being asked to notice the sensation of their stomachs rising and falling with the breath. Activities like these can have long-lasting developmental benefits when practices early and regularly.

Breathe: A Breathing Exercise for Mindful Eating and Digestion

• • • • • • • • • • • • • • • •

Before each meal, encourage your family (or just yourself, if you happen to be eating solo) to take deep breaths before eating. This activity can assist in calming the nervous system, shifting you into rest-and-digest mode. It can also be a good for young kids as a transition from premeal activities to sitting down to eat. This rested state supports your body in digesting food and absorbing the nutrients from what you're eating.

Age Range: 3+

Directions

- Find a comfortable seated position on the floor, at your desk, or at the table.

- Remove any distractions: turn off televisions, turn your cell phone to silent, turn off desktop email notifications.

- Place your hands on your lap or on your belly.

- If comfortable, close your eyes. If not, look down toward your knees or the food before you.

- Take a deep inhale through your nose, filling your belly.

- Pause and then exhale all the air out your mouth.

- Continue until you've completed ten breathing cycles.

- Pick up your utensils and try to have at least three mindful bites free of distractions.

Breathe: A Breathing Exercise to Comfort Yourself and Your Crying Baby

• • • • • • • • • • • • • •

Your newborn is sensitive to the state you approach them in. If you act nervous or frustrated, your baby may become fussy. They often mirror behaviors and emotions. To help calm a crying baby, it's ideal to strive to feel calmness first within yourself. As a parent, I know firsthand this can be easier said than done. But I encourage you to give this grounding breath work a try.

Age Range: Parents of young babies

Directions

- Close your eyes.

- Inhale deeply through your nose for four counts.

- Hold and suspend the breath gently for seven counts.

- Exhale the breath through the nose for eight counts.

- Continue for as many cycles of deep, slow, and steady breaths as it takes to feel more relaxed or that time allows.

- If at any point you no longer feel grounded or become frustrated while comforting your baby, kiss your baby to show loving-kindness to both your baby and yourself as you forgive yourself once you regain control and feel grounded again.

- As you do this breathing exercise, remind yourself that mindfulness practice is a learning process, so leave self-judgment and criticism by the wayside.

Breathe: A Breathing Exercise for Feeding Your Newborn

• • • • • • • • • • • • • • • •

Feeding your baby, whether by breast or bottle, becomes the new constant when you have a newborn. It's easy to fall into the trap of taking that time to scroll through your social media feeds. I know I fell into this routine in the early days with my firstborn. To avoid this trap, use the ten- to forty-five-minute feeding sessions as a time to energize your body and truly tune in to the present moment with this breathing exercise:

Age Range: Parents and babies

Directions

- Inhale four short and steady sips of air through your nose.

- Exhale through your nose in one deep breath out.

- Repeat this exercise until you feel invigorated.

Upgrade: For an extra boost, parents can integrate peppermint, lemon, orange, frankincense, or bergamot essential oil into the breathing exercise.

Breathe: A Breathing Exercise for Preparing for a Nap

• • • • • • • • • • • • • •

Deep, uninterrupted sleep becomes something of the past for many parents with newborns (or toddlers, for that matter). This doesn't mean you can't feel well rested. The key is to listen to your body and make the most of the periods of time you *do* have to sleep. After all, every moment is valuable; if it takes you forty-five minutes to fall asleep, that's forty-five fewer minutes of rest you have.

Age Range: Parents with young children

Directions

- Plug your right nostril by pressing your right thumb on its side. Extend the rest of your fingers straight up.

- Take in a long, deep breath through your left nostril for the count of 4. Hold it for the count of 4, and then exhale for a count of 4.

- Recite the following affirmation silently or aloud:

    - "I will receive the exact amount of rest for my mind and body to be clear, energized, and alert."

The three-minute breathing space is a technique used in many mindfulness-based interventions in the psychology world. This is not an exercise in breathing but in shifting your attention to the breath. In this practice, you'll be using the breath as an anchor to train yourself in attention.

The intention of this exercise is to gather the scattered mind and relate more skillfully to difficult emotions as they arise, even if you're in the kitchen preparing your family's breakfast amidst complaints, competing requests, and email notifications ringing—you get it. Because it's not always possible to close your eyes and meditate for forty minutes. This exercise bridges the gap between extended formal meditation (body scan, sitting meditation) and everyday life, where you really *need* the mindfulness skills.

Age Range: Parents

Directions

- **Make the time.** Choose three times or time frames (such as after waking, at lunch, and before dinner) per day to do this three-minute breathing space. It's best to try to stick to the same times each day. Share these times with your family to create expectations not only of yourself but also of them to provide the space and time you need.

  - **Mama's Breathing Space**
      Time 1: _____ Time 2: _____ Time 3: _____

  - **Papa's Breathing Space**
      Time 1: _____ Time 2: _____ Time 3: _____

- **Position yourself.** Prepare by getting into an erect, dignified posture (sitting or standing). Close your eyes or keep them open with a softened gaze.

- **Check in with your current experience.** Take one minute to notice (1) thoughts going through your mind, (2) pleasant and unpleasant emotions, and (3) body sensations head to toe.

- **Breath focus.** Next, focus on the physical sensations of your breath, following it all the way in and all the way out.

  - Noticing the expansion with each inhale, and the falling back with each exhale. Take several long, slow, deep breaths. Breathe in through your nose fully and out through your nose or mouth fully.

  - Allow your breath to find its own natural rhythm.

  - Bring your full attention to noticing each in-breath as it enters your nostrils, travels down to your lungs, and causes your belly to expand. Notice each out-breath as your belly contracts and air moves up through the lungs back up through the nostrils or mouth.

- Notice how the inhale is different from the exhale. You may experience the air as cool as it enters your nose and warm as you exhale.

- **Expand your awareness.** Expand the field of your awareness around your breathing so it includes a sense of your body as a whole, your posture, and your facial expression.

- **Notice when you lose focus.** Your attention will wander from your breathing to body sensations, thoughts, and emotions.

  - **Mind**: When your mind wanders to thoughts, plans, or problems, simply watch the thought as it enters your awareness as neutrally as you can. Then practice letting go of the thought with your next exhale, as if it was a cloud you were blowing out of a big blue sky.

  - **Body**: You might become distracted by pain or discomfort in the body or twitching or itching sensations that draw your attention away from your breath. If you do, simply follow your awareness there by breathing into it on your inhale. Breathe out the sensations.

  - **Heart**: You may also notice feelings arising, perhaps sadness or happiness, frustration or contentment. Acknowledge whatever comes up, including thoughts or stories about your experience. Simply notice where your mind went without judging it, pushing it away, clinging to it, or wishing it were different. Simply refocus your mind and guide your attention back to your breath.

- **Close your practice.** As this practice comes to an end, slowly allow your attention to expand and notice your entire body and then beyond your body to the room you are in. When you're ready, open your eyes and come back fully alert. Carry these moments of expanded awareness to the rest of your day.

- **Set an intention, and make time for reflection.** Set your intention to use this practice three times each day to help cultivate and strengthen attention. After two weeks of practicing the three-minute breathing space, reflect on one thing you or your partner learned from or gained from the exercise.

Breathe: The Breathing Ball for Kids

• • • • • • • • • • • • • • • • •

The goal of this exercise is to encourage your child to have mindful awareness of breath in a fun and playful way.

Materials

- Hoberman sphere or balloon

Age Range: 4–12

Directions

- **Engage.** Say something like this to your child:

    - "Let's play a breathing game together. Did you know that breathing can change the way you feel? Sometimes I take deep breaths to help me calm down and feel happy."

- **Find an appropriate space.** Encourage your child to choose a space you have dedicated to mindfulness practice, the garden, or another area where you'll have limited distractions.

- **Mindful movement before breathing.** Demonstrate while instructing:

    - "Now let's stand up nice and tall. Press your feet into the earth and lengthen through the spine. Let's begin with shoulder circles, taking our shoulders up to the ears and back and down. Do this two more times. Breathe in and lift the shoulders up to the ears, and breathe out as you bring your shoulders down. One more time."

- **Demonstrate use of breathing tool.** Get out a balloon or a Hoberman sphere. Demonstrate taking big, deep belly breaths, either filling and emptying a balloon and the belly, or expanding and contracting the Hoberman sphere in sync with your breath. Say:

    - "Now begin to watch the breathing ball, or close your eyes and begin. Breathing in, let the belly puff up, and breathing out, let the belly move back toward the spine. Again, breathing in and out. Six more times. Inhaling and exhaling. Five more …"

- **Reflect.** Take a moment to ask your child how her or his body and mind feel after taking eight deep breaths, while sharing your own experiences.

- **Allow for autonomy.** Open up the opportunity for your child to now teach you or a sibling to use the breathing tool.

- **Encourage practice.** Share with your children that whenever they feel frustrated, angry, or nervous, they can come back to their breath to find a calm, still, and happy place.

Meditate

Meditate: Introduction

• • • • • • • • • • • • • • • •

For many, the mindfulness journey begins by introducing informal mindfulness activities into the daily routine. Once you've started to add awareness to daily activities, like nursing, eating, running, and drinking coffee, you may start to work in time for meditation.

Fitting Meditation into the Parenting Game

Parents juggle myriad responsibilities: managing kids, jobs, community obligations, school meetings, yoga classes, cleaning, chauffeuring. Mamas and papas have such busy lives that it may seem impossible to find a quiet place to meditate, even for short periods of time. But no matter how many kids and responsibilities you have, there's *always* room in your schedule for meditation; it just requires a bit of creativity in figuring out how, when, and where to meditate.

Parents sometimes meditate at strange times and in strange places, and that's okay. It may be on a pillow in the bedroom first thing in the morning, at the kitchen table while their children nap, in the car pool lane, or when stuck in gridlock traffic (a renowned psychologist I attended a seminar with recently mentioned the "taillight meditation" he does every day in his hour-long commute between home to work). We can use whatever time that's available to use, wherever and whenever that may be, and however that looks: sitting, walking, lying down.

Show up and Anchor Yourself

The hardest part of meditation is said to be showing up. When you make the effort to show up and meditate for yourself, you're meditating for your children too. Choose an anchor for your attention, whether that's your breath, your mantra, an object in front of you, or a visualization.

Get Comfortable, then Get Comfortable with Being Uncomfortable

If your meditation practice is uncomfortable, or you're distracted or interrupted, simply notice what happened instead of getting caught up in your own judgments. Make an observation, such as "Hmmm, my body is uncomfortable today" or "My mind is distracted today" or "Looks like today's practice is a short one," and leave it at that. No judgment. Just the facts. When you become a witness to your thoughts, emotions, and experiences, you're less likely to fall into the judgment trap, which is where you will struggle most.

Am I Doing It Right?

Let go of expectations that you will be able to have clear focus during meditation. There is no perfect or right way to meditate. You may fidget. You may cough. You may open your eyes to check your timer or clock. It bears repeating: just show up.

Meditate: Seated Meditation for Teens and Adults

• • • • • • • • • • • • • • • •

Mindfulness meditation couldn't be simpler. Just take a seat and choose an anchor for your attention, be it breath, body sensations, mantra, or an object in front of you such as a candle. Your attention will wander. Each time it does, note where it goes and kindly guide yourself back to the focus of your awareness in the here-and-now.

Age Range: 12+

Directions

- Check out this infographic. You can copy it and put up in your mindful space in the house or take a photo of it with your cell phone to carry with you wherever your daily adventures take you.

Explore: A mala can be a tool to remind you to practice mindfulness, but it's also a tool for mindfulness practice via breathing exercises or mantra repetition. Make your own mala bracelet or necklace; visit pages 126-127 to learn how.

Science: There are hundreds of research studies into the benefits of mindfulness meditation for all ages. For example, research has shown adults start to reap the benefits of formal meditation practice with as little as twelve minutes per day, five days a week. Hundreds of brain imaging studies have shown meditation at this rate literally changes the structure and function of the brain.

Guided Meditations

Using these instructions, you can practice mindfulness meditation on your own anytime and anywhere. However, listening to guided meditations can also be helpful, especially if you are new to meditation or have had a day that has you struggling to wind down for a meditation practice! Instructions from an experienced teacher can help remind us to come back to the present moment, let go of distracting thoughts and not be so hard on ourselves. Check out apps like "Insight Timer" or "Calm" or "Headspace".

Eyes

Choose what you'd like to do with your eyes. If you're feeling particularly anxious or you want to anchor into the space you're in, keep your eyes slightly open, looking downward 45 degrees). If you are comfortable, softly close your eyes.

Mouth

Trying wearing a half smile, just as you see images of Buddha wearing. This may encourage you to not take things too seriously, and engage in curious awareness instead!

Breathe

Notice your natural breathing pattern with curious awareness when you get into your desired position. You can anchor into the body sensations that are most prominent with breathing (such as cool air entering nose on the inhale, warm air on exhale; rising and falling of the tummy), or observe and follow each round of inhale and exhale. Make no effort to control your breath.

Arms and Hands

Relax your shoulders and arms. Let your hands rest on your thighs, knees, or one hand inside another in your lap. For nursing moms, you can try placing a cushion or nursing pillow on your lap to rest your hands on to relieve stress of the upper back.

Emotions

Just as you do when thought watching, heart watch. Notice emotions that emerge during meditation. Notice the experience of that emotion — from thoughts to body sensations — then kindly hold your heart's hand as you guide your attention back to your anchor, your breath.

Thoughts

Mindfulness meditation isn't about letting your thoughts wander. But it isn't about trying to empty your mind, either. Rather, the practice involves paying close attention to the present moment. When you notice your mind wandering — and it will from time to time! — notice the patterns of thought that emerge with curious awareness, file those thoughts away for later retrieval, then gently guide yourself back to your breath with your next inhale.

Body Sensations

You may get an incurable itch or feel restless in stillness. This is normal. If this is distracting you, just notice the sensations, breath into them, and if you need to adjust your position or scratch a toe, then do so!

Time

Start with a few minutes at a time once per day, working up in frequency or duration. the plethora of benefits of mindfulness meditation with as little as 12 minutes daily! You can use a time on your phone, kitchen timer, or your no-longer-napping baby's cry for you as your signal for the end of your meditation!

Position Yourself

Choose your body position — lying down (bed, floor), standing (outdoors or indoors), or seated (in chair or on a cushion or rolled yoga mat or towel). For lying down, relax with legs straight, feet flopped to the sides, palms up. If standing, stand with confidence, feet slightly apart, with legs descending like roots from a tree grounding to the surface below. For seated, sit in a chair or on a cushion always ensuring your spine is straight and not strained, and that your knees are below your hips. If in a chair, place your feet flat on the floor. If you're sitting cross-legged on a cushion. You can always make a higher seat with a cushion or towel!

Meditate: Seated Meditation for Children

• • • • • • • • • • • • • •

Make remembering the basics of mindful meditation easy for kids by teaching them the seven S's of seated practice: sit up straight, sit silently, sense the breath, sit still, shut eyes or stare, scan the heart and mind, start short and simple.

Make it fun, not a chore or a punishment. It's as simple as sitting still and straight. Explain to your children that meditation is a way to help them relax and enjoy whatever they're doing in their life. Use scripts from this book to guide the mindfulness practice, or apps like Calm, Headspace, or Mindful Powers.

It's important to share with your child that there's no right or wrong way to meditate. Mamas and papas, you need to also remind *yourselves* of this as well, as you support your child in mindfulness practice. Frequency is key to seeing benefits over time. Do encourage their curiosity, efforts, and willingness to practice, even if just briefly. Consider building it into your child's evening routine.

Age Range: 3–12

Directions

- Check out this infographic. You can copy it and hang it up in your child's mindful space.

Guided Meditations

Using these instructions, you can can use the 7 S's to support your child's seated meditation practice. Explain to your child that meditation is a way to help them relax and enjoy whatever they're doing in their life. Use scripts from this book to guide the mindfulness practice, or apps like "Calm", "Headspace", or "Mindful Powers".

Sit up Straight

Ask your child to sit up straight, but relaxed.

Shut Eyes or Stare

Give your child the option to close their eyes, or gaze at something ahead of them, such as the flame of a burning candle.

Sit Silently

If this is a challenge, try turning this practice into a game of "who can be the quietest". When the silence is broken, break silence with words of love and kindness, as opposed to judgement or criticism.

Scan the Heart + Mind

In a gentle way, guide your child in noticing emotion(s) they currently feel and the thoughts in their mind -- both pleasant and unpleasant emotions and thoughts! Encourage your child to not feel bad about noticing feelings or ideas that pop up while sitting, just encourage them to come to their breathing or gaze of the candle to come back to the mindfulness practice.

Sense the Breath

Encourage your child to investigate where they FEEL their breath, whether it's the nose, mouth, throat, chest, or belly. Challenge them to take deep belly breaths. The first few times you sit for mindfulness practice, try guiding a breath exercise. First ask them to inhale through the nose filling the belly with the breath, to hold their breath while you count to two, and then breathe out through the mouth while you count to four. Pause briefly, then repeat.

Start Short + Simple

Don't get too caught up in meeting a set time frame when introducing your child to seated meditation. As little as a few minutes of daily mindfulness practice is profoundly beneficial for children! Use a timer your child sets or a guided meditation by yourself, another child, or an app

Sit Still

Sitting still may not come naturally at first for your child. Don't get upset if they're fidgety. Expect it! In the introduction phase, you can encourage them to sit cross legged, rock back and forth a few times to find their centre in stillness. Encourage them to try their best to relax and focus on their breath. With regular practice, your child will be able to sit still longer.

Meditate: Family Meditation

• • • • • • • • • • • • • •

It's valuable for parents to create their own meditation practice, but developing a family meditation practice can support your family in becoming more positive and getting along better with each other and those in the world.

Age Range: All ages

Directions

- **Wake up the senses with scent and sound.** Engage your children in lighting candles or choosing oils for a diffuser for the meditation session. Have your children take turns ringing bells (or choose some other audible cue) to signal the start of the meditation.

- **Yoga.** Taking time for mindful movements, such as a few yoga stretches, is a pleasant way to calm mind and body before meditation.

- **Mindful sip before you sit.** Bringing in cups of tea or hot cocoa for family meditation sessions can help set the tone. Simply be together for a few moments to bring about family intimacy that children and adults alike benefit from.

- **Get into position.** Have your family sit in a circle on cushions, pillows, or yoga mats. Gently encourage a good posture. Children should be given a choice of whether they want to close their eyes or gaze softly at the floor in front of them.

- **Breathe.** Encourage family members to feel their breath going in and out, filling their belly.

- **Minutes for mindfulness.** Plan to sit together for two to ten minutes, depending on ages and abilities. Always remember it's completely normal for younger children to be restless, and simply being still and quiet for a few minutes is beneficial for them.

- **End mindfully.** Allow your children to take turns ringing a bell, playing a singing bowl, or blowing out the candles to signal the end of the family meditation practice. Encourage your children to remain quiet and still until they can no longer hear the sound of the bell or bowl or see the smoke of the blown-out flame.

- **Mindful sip before you move.** Take a moment to enjoy your tea or hot cocoa together before the family speeds off in all directions.

Meditate: Nourishing Morning Meditation

• • • • • • • • • • • • •

Mamas and papas, it's time to find grounding in your daily grounds (or tea leaves). Start the day slowly sipping your desired beverage, free of tech devices and to-do lists. The morning coffee and tea meditation is a mindful moment that may support you in boosting focus, improving attention, and help you better cope with challenges you may face day-to-day at work and home.

It will facilitate a more restful, rejuvenating state rather than waking up and first thing checking email or answering the demands of hungry littles right out the gates, resulting in stress flowing through your veins before you've even broken your fast from the night.

Age Range: Parents

Directions

- **Set your alarm.** Set your alarm before your family usually wakes up. Ensure said alarm is not a cell phone that you then immediately start scrolling emails or social media on. If you must use your phone, then put it on airplane mode.

- **Sit.** Start by sitting down in a chair, with your back straight, feet firmly grounded to the floor. Either close your eyes or look down at about a 45 degree angle.

- **Be Here Now.** Remind yourself you have nowhere else to be. This moment is a gift. You're going to drink your coffee slowly and reverently, as if it's the axis on which the earth revolves, as Thich Nhat Hanh would say. Your to-do lists can and surely will wait.

- **Breathe.** Take ten deep inhales through your nose, exhaling through your mouth. Notice the gap between each inhale and exhale; pause. This slow and deep breathing shifts you from the sympathetic (fight-or-flight) to parasympathetic (rest-and-digest) nervous system.

- **Open up to Your Experience.** Open your eyes. Wrap both hands around your mug of coffee, cup of tea, or glass of water. Engage all your senses in the drinking experience.

- **Tap into Your Senses.** First focus on the sensations of touch. Notice the temperature of your beverage and the aromas in your nose. Notice any memories they may bring up. Your sense of smell is unique among the senses, as it's unfiltered before going to your brain. The olfactory system is tied to your memory center, so your scent memory is a powerful force. Perhaps you're brought back to your parents brewing coffee on Christmas morning or late-night study dates with friends in university. Follow where your mind goes, and then gently guide it back to this cup of coffee in this moment.

- **Raise a Cup or Glass.** Now mindfully bring your cup up to your mouth. Notice the muscles and joints helping raise the cup to your mouth.

- **First Mindful Sip.** Finally, sip. Notice the first bursts of flavor in your mouth, the temperature, the texture. If your mind goes to the next sip, gently guide it back to the current sip. Follow the liquid as it goes down your throat to your stomach and enters your cells.

- **Practice Gratitude.** Last, but not least, express a sense of gratitude for all those who made this beverage possible. Do not forget gratitude to yourself for making the time and space for a mindful moment.

- **Breathe and Be Mindful.** Take a cleansing breath and move onto your next sips, and the rest of your day, mindfully.

Upgrade: Looking for something to fill your vessel for this exercise? You've got options. Check out the Better Butter Coffee recipe on page 162. Or the WaterFull recipe on page 160.

Meditate: Half-Smile Meditation

• • • • • • • • • • • • • • • •

This is easy to implement in moments when things get tense between family members, at work or school, or stuck in gridlock traffic. It's a simple exercise of cracking a half-smile to shift your mood state, or grinning and (mindfully) bearing it.

Age Range: 8+

Directions

- **Crack a half-smile.** Just a baby one. It's hard not to go into a big toothy grin, isn't it?

- **Half-smile during your seated meditation.** You may want to consider bringing this exercise into your body scan or meta-meditation by beginning with a half-smile on your face. After all, meditation isn't a grim activity. Instead, it's meant to be supportive; meditation should give you a mind-set more like "Wow, I get to meditate, spend time with myself, and cultivate a relationship with myself."

- **Smiling mantra for meditation.** Try reciting words inspired by Thich Nhat Hanh: "Breathing in, I calm my body. Breathing out, I smile. Dwelling in the present moment, I know this is a wonderful moment."

Science: This is a good activity to help us check in with ourselves, not take ourselves so seriously. It's good for if you're feeling annoyed or stressed. A half-smile during practice sends a message to the brain you're happy, and it reduces stress.

Meditate: Family Singing Bowl Activity

• • • • • • • • • • • • • • • • •

Singing bowls, bells that are capable of producing a sustained musical note, date back to 560 BC. While often found in shrines and temples, the singing bowl can be a mainstay in any family home. Singing bowls produce sounds that invite us to enter into the present moment. The exercises introduced here are designed to be fun and interactive ways you can help your children learn mindfulness, meditate, and improve their concentration levels. For teens and adults, the sounds may invoke a deep state of relaxation to help enter into meditation.

Age Range: 2+

Directions

- **Listening practice.** Help your children find the Ss as they first engage with the singing bowl:

    - Sit silently.

    - Sit up straight.

    - Sit still.

    - Sense your breathing.

    - Shut your eyes and tap into sense of hearing as you listen to the singing bowl.

- **Breathing with the bell.** This exercise is about focusing on breathing and sound.

    - Come to a seated position on a cushion, couch, chair, the floor, the grass. Eyes can be open or closed.

    - When the bell is singing, you and your children can listen to it.

    - Encourage breathing with the sound, following the sound into the body to feel the energy within.

    - Some parents like to encourage children to raise their hand when they no longer hear the sound.

    - The bell is usually invited to sing three times, but you can choose to do it for more or less.

    - You can also do this with a regular bell.

- **Inviting the bell to sing.** The singing bowl is a gift that we can practice inviting into our family member's hearts.

  - Come to a seated position on a cushion, couch, chair, the floor, the grass, with your eyes open.

  - Parents, rest the bowl in the palm of one hand. Have the fingers stretched out as if they were petals of a flower opened in full bloom.

  - With your other hand, carefully lift the "bell inviter" (the wooden mallet used to invite the bell to sing). Your role is to show your children we are not hitting the bell, but rather, kindly inviting the bell to sing.

  - As you all focus on the breath, repeat a little poem to the bell:

    Breathing in, I open my heart to the bell.

    Breathing out, I ask the bell to sing and bring peace to my heart and the hearts of all others.

  - Demonstrate or instruct your child to bring the mallet gently to the bell to awaken it again by gently touching it. Next, take the mallet more firmly to the bell to hear it sing.

- **Namaste.** This exercise is a great tool to close a mindful movement or meditation or breathing practice, with the family or on your own.

  - The singing bowl sits in front of a family member, who rings the bell.

  - Those present are encouraged to focus on taking deep breaths.

  - Bring hands into Namaste (palms facing and touching, hands at the center of the chest, which is the energy of the heart center).

  - Bow to the bell, acknowledging the peaceful energy of the bell to those present.

Explore: We can use the day-to-day noises in our environment for mindfulness of listening exercises: the school bell, an emergency vehicle siren, the ring of a cell phone, a doorbell, a bird singing, the chords of a guitar, the keys of a piano. Choose one to work with and, when hearing it, pause, close the eyes, and notice the breath and sound.

Upgrade: Use the singing bowl as part of your family's reward system (see page 36). You can recognize your children as the bell master for their kindness to others, good behavior, receiving tokens on a reward chart, or the most progress in their schoolwork. The bell master is the person who is responsible for inviting the bell to sing.

Meditate: Body Scan Meditation

• • • • • • • • • • • • • • • •

The body scan meditation is an exercise in observing that is intended to heighten your awareness of your body in a systematic way. You will be observing each part of your body passively, just noticing, without the need to make any changes or cause anything to occur. You can simply watch and take note of any changes that happen on their own, without any effort on your part.

It can be supportive to do a body scan mindfulness meditation exercise daily for ten minutes or longer. As you engage in this practice regularly, you will become more highly attuned to what's happening in your body.

Age Range: Teens and adults

Directions

- **Choose your guide.** You have options, whether you want to self-guide or listen to a guided body scan you can easily find on a mindfulness app, iTunes, Spotify, or YouTube.

- **Protect your mindfulness practice.** When doing a body scan, especially if you're doing a longer one, you may need to ask colleagues or family members to respect the boundaries of the space and time you need to dedicate to your practice.

- **Get into position.** This meditation can be done sitting or lying. If sitting, allow your feet to become firmly planted on the ground and sit up confidently but not stiffly. If lying down, allow your backside to find points of contact with the ground below, with your palms facing up and legs relaxed. Eyes can be closed or eyelids softened.

- **Breathe.** Take a few deep belly breaths and then allow your breathing to come into its natural rhythm, without any conscious effort to change your breathing.

- **Scan your body for sensations.** Start your body scan at your toes, just noticing how they feel. Are they tense? Cold? Hot? Focus your attention here for a few breaths before moving on to the soles of your feet.

- **Move up toward your head.** Repeat the process as you travel from your feet to your ankles, calves, knees, and thighs. Continue to move up your hips, lower back, stomach, chest, shoulders, arms, hands, neck, and head—maintaining your focus on each body part as you notice sensations.

- **Breathe as you body scan.** Breathe into areas that are holding stress and try to release it.

- **Allow for pause.** If you notice anything of interest, you may choose to allow your attention to linger there for a moment as you observe how your muscles and tissues are feeling.

- **Scan the body as a whole.** After you reach the top of your head, keep the attitude of passive observation as you mentally scan your body now as a whole. Do a complete scan, at your own pace, from your feet to your head.

- **Wrap up your body scan.** You're now fully aware of how your body is feeling and have completed a body scan. Notice how you're feeling now, mentally and physically. Observe any changes that may have occurred, all on their own. Conclude the body scan, and allow yourself to become fully alert and energized with three deep breaths. Flutter your eyes open.

- **Try the brief body scan.** You can follow the body scan instructions or listen to five- or ten-minute body scans in your favorite app before, during, and toward the end of your training sessions, competitions, presentations, and more. Why? A brief body scan allows you to check in with your body sensations and alignment.

Meditate: Eye of the Storm Meditation

· · · · · · · · · · · · ·

This script is one that can be read by parents to partners or to kids of all ages. The focus is on a storm and oneself in the center of the storm, emphasizing that whatever comes up in life, no matter how chaotic, there is a calm, quiet place in the center of us that cannot be touched. With breath as our anchor, we can find that space. This assists all ages with coping with stress in the moment and when faced with challenges in the future.

Age Range: Teens and adults

Directions

- **Choose your guide.** You can self-guide or have a family member guide you with the instructions below.
- **Get into position.** This meditation can be done standing, sitting, or lying down. If sitting or standing, allow your feet to become firmly planted on the ground and have your back confident, but not stiff. Allow the hands to fall where comfortable. If lying down, allow your backside to find points of contact with the ground below, with your palms facing up and legs relaxed. Eyes can be closed or eyelids softened.
- **Breathe.** Take a few deep belly breaths and then allow your breathing to come into its natural rhythm, without any conscious effort to change your breathing.
- **Check in with your stress.** Check in with yourself; are you feeling stress at this moment? See this stress in your mind's eye. Imagine that stress is like having a tornado in your life. You can see the chaos this storm brings. But you have your breath. Breathe in and out. You are safe.
- **Notice the eye of the storm.** Now imagine you are looking from a satellite above the earth; you can see within the tornado, and you notice there is an eye to this storm: a calm, still center.
- **Drop into the storm.** You are now dropping into the center of the storm. You see it wreaking havoc all around you, and yet, you're calm and peaceful.
- **See your stress in the storm.** Within this tornado, see the stressors—big or small—in your life swirling around you. You are simply observing with all your senses. There are situations, people, to dos that could stress you out. But they don't, for you're feeling calm and peaceful.
- **Breathe through the stressors.** If your breathing has halted or become shallow, bring yourself back to the deep, natural breathing rhythm you started with.
- **You have the choice to get caught up in the stress storm or not.** Coming back to the eye of the storm, you see you always have the choice to move into the storm and experience chaotic stress that can swirl up in one's life or not. You can be in the eye of the storm at any moment, at any moment, or in any situation. You always have a choice whether to observe and respond, or become reactionary and overwhelmed when stress happens in your life. Simply breathe deeply in the eye of the storm.
- **Practice.** You can practice this meditation anytime, anywhere, in any position. You may be observing a stressor with your eyes open and dropping back into that experience of being in the calm, relaxed eye of the stress storm. Or do this to start or end the day, to check in with your stressors or break thought patterns that may set your day off on the wrong tone or keep you up at night.

Meditate: Mandala Colouring Page

• • • • • • • • • • • • • •

"The quieter you become, the more you are able to hear."

—Rumi

Meditate: Partner Meditation

• • • • • • • • • • • • • • • •

You can choose any meditation to do with your partner. In our house, we occasionally do evening body scans in bed, when we get our young children to bed at a decent time, almost as a reward to ourselves. But that's us. You and your partner can get creative and check out apps that offer meditations based on time frames or topics.

Age Range: Adults

Directions

- **Choose your meditation.** Perhaps it's a moment to savor silence and just be present with each other and yourself in a seated silent meditation. Or perhaps a guided meditation from your favorite app. Choose your own mindful adventure with your partner.

- **Choose your position.** Sit or lay down beside each other or sit facing one another.

- **Compassionate touch.** Meditating seated together with knees touching or lying side-by-side holding hands are ways to physically connect for your mindful moment. You can even take it a step further and get a cream or essential oil to massage each other's shoulders, hands, arms, or scalp, bringing awareness to the texture, temperature, and sense of connectedness while doing so.

- **Engage the senses.** Get creative with this one. Have a candle or diffuser going to tap into the sense of smell. Have a cup of tea to engage all the senses to start your mindfulness practice.

- **Get grateful.** What a gift, to get to sit down with your partner for a mindful moment. Express gratitude for yourself and your partner for making the time to practice.

Meditate: Grounding Meditation

• • • • • • • • • • • • • • • •

This meditation supports drawing awareness to your breath, body, and surroundings. Earth has an incredibly grounding nature about it. Running, walking, hiking, gardening, swimming in the ocean, relaxing on the beach are just a few activities that can tune you into the natural energy of the earth. Grounding—or getting your mind and body connected when facing stressors—enables you to model effective and appropriate ways of dealing with strong emotions and situations for your friends, colleagues, family, and children.

You can do this exercise alone, with your partner, with your child or teen, or with the whole family.

Age Range: 7+

Directions

- **Get into position.** This meditation can be done sitting or standing. Whether sitting or standing, allow your feet to become firmly planted on the ground and have your back confident. Allow your hands to rest on your lap (if sitting) or relaxed by your side (if standing). If standing, take what is referred to as the mountain pose in yoga, with your feet descending to the ground, hip-width distance apart. Eyes can be closed or eyelids softened.

- **Breathe.** Take three deep breaths. Focus on the flow of your breath as it goes in and out.

- **Visualize your body as a tree.** Imagine your body is a tree, any type or size of tree you wish, with leaves, without leaves, tall, or short.

- **Grow your roots.** Once you can picture your body as a tree, imagine your tree growing roots deep into the ground. The roots may appear like traditional tree roots or anything you imagine. It's your tree, after all. Perhaps the roots are beams of colorful light, or roots that sparkle with glitter and diamonds. Have your tree represent *you*.

- **Your roots reach down to the earth's core.** Grow your tree roots down deep into the earth, to the very core, where the grounding will be strongest. To help visualize this, imagine a cross section of the planet, with you standing or sitting on the surface. Picture your roots reaching down to the core.

- **Mentally repeat a personalized mantra.** Once you see your roots have made a connection to the earth's core, mentally repeat a personalized mantra for release. For example, "I release … [whatever fits for you in the moment, whether fear, tension, stress, anxiety, guilt, anger]." As you say this, visualize stress and tension exiting your body through your roots. Tune into your breath and repeat your mantra until you feel clear.

- **Breathe and reflect.** Open your eyes when you are ready. Take a few moments of silence. Breathe. Notice how you feel mentally and physically after this visualization.

Meditate: Thought Clouds

• • • • • • • • • • • • • • • •

Thoughts are like clouds. They float by, always moving, shifting. This is a visualization exercise focused around clouds to guide your child through. The intention is to practice focus and observation, ease worry and distress, and bring on a state of relaxation for the child. Experiences will vary.

Age Range: All ages

Directions

- **Get into position.** Encourage your child to lie down, whether on a couch, bed, floor, yoga mat, or grassy spot outside.

- **Watch the clouds above.** If weather permits, I highly encourage you to lay down on a grassy spot and look up at the clouds with your child. This can be a relaxing activity. Engage your child in this focusing activity as you both watch the clouds overhead move and shift continually. This doesn't have to be done in silence. Just encourage attention and curiosity.

- **Breathe.** Take a few deep belly breaths and then allow your breathing to come into its natural rhythm.

- **Let thoughts come into your mind.** Mindfulness isn't about erasing thoughts in your mind. Notice thoughts as they come in. Let each thought float around in your head like a cloud, letting it be there so that you can observe how it makes you feel.

- **Choose what to do with your thought.** Now is your chance to decide if this thought is something that's important to you or one you want to let go of.

- **Continue observing thought clouds.** Try this with another thought that comes to mind. Observe it floating, then decide what you'd like to do with it. Just like clouds in the sky, thoughts may look like scary creatures like a dragon at first, but if we pause and watch, it can transform.

- **Reflect.** Parents, you may want to reflect on the thought clouds with your child. It can be a good time to evaluate bothersome thought patterns.

- **Practice.** This exercise can be helpful to regularly check in with thought patterns. If something comes to mind that doesn't make you feel good, do the thought cloud activity to decide if you want the thought to float away or can see it from a different perspective.

Meditate: Loving-Kindness Meditation

• • • • • • • • • • • • • •

Loving-kindness is a meditation focused on nurturing compassion, kindness, goodwill, and love for oneself and others. Loving-kindness meditations (LKMs) teach you how to let go of judgment, speak more compassionately, and accept yourself, your partner, and your children just as you and they are. Repeat this loving-kindness meditation as often as possible.

The traditional LKM sees you first send love and kindness to yourself, then to those you hold dear, like family and friends, next to people you may not hold dear, and then to the universe. In the end, the universe sends all that love you sent out back again to you. You can adapt this script for younger children by choosing one line reflecting loving-kindness, such as "May I/they be happy and healthy."

Age Range: Teens and adults (can be adapted for younger children)

Directions

- **Get into position.** Close your eyes. Sit comfortably with your feet flat on the floor and your spine straight. Relax your whole body. Keep your eyes closed throughout the whole visualization and bring your awareness inward. Breathe comfortably.

- **Send loving-kindness to yourself.** Say these words silently to yourself, reminding yourself you deserve this kind of care as you repeat:

  > May I be happy, healthy, and peaceful.
  > May I let go of sadness and bad feelings
  > May I be free from pain and suffering.
  > May I be filled with loving-kindness.

- **Send loving-kindness to your family.** Continue to breathe. As you breathe, imagine you're unleashing a power you have stored up inside of you to your family. The power comes from your heart. You're breathing out the warmth and glow to everyone you love in your family. Imagine their faces. Say these words silently yourself:

  > I spread this loving-kindness out.
  > I send love to my family.
  > May they be happy, healthy, and peaceful.
  > May they let go of sadness and bad feelings.
  > May they be free from pain and suffering.
  > May they be filled with loving-kindness.

- **Send loving-kindness to close friends.** As you breathe, feel the love and kindness filling your heart. Imagine you are glowing with the energy of love. You will now spread this energy to your friends and colleagues. Say these words silently to yourself:

> I spread this loving-kindness out.
> I send love to my closest friends and colleagues.
> May they be happy, healthy, and peaceful.
> May they let go of sadness and bad feelings.
> May they be free from pain and suffering.
> May they be filled with loving-kindness.

- **Send loving-kindness to a neutral person in your life.** Next, think about someone you may see regularly but don't know well. Examples could include a grocery store clerk, a barista at a local coffee shop, or a neighbor. Bring this person to mind now. Say these words silently to yourself:

> I spread this loving-kindness out.
> I send love to someone who has once made me feel bad.
> May they be happy, healthy, and peaceful.
> May they let go of sadness and bad feelings.
> May they be free from pain and suffering.
> May they be filled with loving-kindness.

- **Send loving-kindness to a difficult person in your life.** Next, think about someone in your family or community who has made you feel bad. Perhaps it's someone you don't like to feel sympathy or compassion for. See this person as a whole being who is deserving of love and kindness, a whole being who feels physical or mental pain and suffering. You have the power to warm their heart, too, and release this bad feeling. Say these words silently to yourself:

> I spread this loving-kindness out.
> I send love to someone who has once made me feel bad.
> May they be happy, healthy, and peaceful.
> May they let go of sadness and bad feelings.
> May they be free from pain and suffering.
> May they be filled with loving-kindness.

- **Send loving-kindness to all being in the entire universe.** Now, you're going to send love in all directions: to a loved one, a neutral person, a difficult person, and all beings everywhere on earth and in every universe. Say these words silently to yourself:

> I send love now to all beings of all kinds in all directions, on earth and in all universes.
> May they be happy, healthy, and peaceful.
> May they be free from suffering.
> May they let go of sadness and bad feelings.
> May they be free from pain and suffering.
> May they be filled with loving-kindness.

- **Receive loving-kindness.** Now, everyone to whom you have sent your love is sending their love back. Say these words silently to yourself:

> May I be happy, healthy, and peaceful.
> May I let go of sadness and bad feelings.
> May I be free from pain and suffering.
> May I be filled with loving-kindness.

- **Breathe and reflect.** Take a deep breath in and breathe out. Take another deep breath in, and let it go. Notice the state of your mind and how you feel after this meditation. Open your eyes when you are ready.

- **Practice.** As with all mindfulness activities, practice is key. Repeat the loving-kindness meditation when you're struggling with envy, stress in family life, comparison with others, or whatever is troubling you. This can help you disengage from that train of thought and bring your mind back to you and the experience of the present moment. LKM can be practiced anywhere. You can use this meditation in a traffic jam, on the bus, and on an airplane. As you silently practice this meditation among people, you will come to feel a wonderful connection with them: the power of lovingkindness.

Science: While the loving-kindness meditation originates in Buddhist traditions, it's now practiced across cultures and is the focus of extensive research by scientists. Here are just a few of the findings:

- It improves our social connections by literally changing the brain. More specifically, the insula and the temporal parietal junction, which are responsible for our ability to empathize, are impacted. It's been shown to strengthen your sense of connection with others and increase positive feelings (Hutcherson, Seppala, and Gross 2008).
- It improves vagal tone (a physiological measurement of resilience and well-being).
- It increases grey matter in the brain responsible for emotional regulation.
- It decreases chronic pain.
- It can decrease symptoms of depression.
- It boosts a wide range of emotions, including joy, gratitude, contentment, pride, interest, hope, amusement, and awe.
- It can have an immediate relaxation effect on the body.
- It makes you more likely to help others.

Move and Play

Move and Play: Introduction

· · · · · · · · · · · · ·

As parents, most days involve a lot of moving and hustling, often done mindlessly. Together, let's explore ways to move and play mindfully.

What Does Mindfully Moving and Playing Look Like?

Movement can be a form of meditation in itself, if you go about it with full awareness. You can be present while your body is going through the motions of walking, driving kids to and from school or practices, cooking, cleaning, getting dressed. This is all part of training your mind to be mindful in day-to-day activities.

Our family has worked mindful movement into our routine with mindful walks and bike rides in the morning and brief breath work or yoga practice after bath time, before books and sleepy time. We do a variety of activities as a family on weekends, such as walking, hiking, running with jogging stroller, bike riding, snowboarding, paddleboarding, and family yoga classes.

Why Bring Mindfulness into Your Move and Play Time?

Bringing mindfulness and presence to movement and play is good for all members of the family. Benefits range from improvement in quality or quantity of sleep, behavior management, confidence, and bodily awareness. Mindful movement can also assist your family members explore limits of discomfort and tune into sensations in body and mind.

Move and Play: Mindful Movement Intention Setting

Children often play and move based on the intrinsic rewards because of sheer enjoyment. Mamas and papas often find themselves exercising as an escape, and then while moving, you get caught up in mental to-do lists, guilt over being away from children, or rehearsing past or future events. Mental activity can take you out of the present experience of movement. This section contains a number physical activities that you can infuse with mindfulness. Before jumping ahead, though, let's take a moment and explore the role of movement in your life right now.

I want to enhance my mindful awareness and focus while moving and playing because:

_____

_____

The physical exercise I'm most mindful during:

_____

_____

The playful activity I'm most mindful during:

_____

_____

What supports me in being most mindful in the activity noted above (e.g., time of day, lighting, indoors vs. outdoors, music):

_____

_____

The physical exercise I want to be more mindful during:

_____

_____

The playful activity I want to be more mindful during:

_____

_____

How I see movement and play being a part of my family's mindfulness journey:

_____

_____

Move and Play: Mindful Training Session

• • • • • • • • • • • • • • • •

Physical activity is something we want to make time for daily, but sometimes, we go to great lengths to carve out time and spend money to access a training facility or class and simply go through the motions of our exercises. Use these practices to bring more appreciation and presence to your next training session.

Age Range: Teens and adults

Directions

- **Get a feel for what you're feeling.** Before you get suited up, get a sense of how you're feeling. Are you feeling anxious? Confident? Annoyed? Take a couple of minutes to sit down and allow your mind to rest pretraining or competition.

- **Just breathe.** How mindful are you of your breath while you train or engage in recreational or competitive sports? As in yoga, breathing is a life force essential for cardiovascular and weight training. Breath can become more forceful when we tire, which fatigues us. Clasp your hands behind your back, open your chest, and take a few deep breaths to help feel more grounded before you begin your training session or competition.

- **Do a brief body scan.** Before, during, and toward the end of your training session or competition, you may want to check in with your body sensations and alignment with a brief body scan. Don't judge or criticize the sensations; just bring awareness to them. Notice what happens when you consciously open your chest with shoulders back and spine straight; does your breath feel different? Check out pages 76-77 to get an idea of what the body scan meditation is all about.

- **Observe your external environment.** Practice a gentle, curious awareness of what's going on around you while training or competing. Whether it's the same gym you always lift at or the same track or trail you run on regularly, take time to notice what's in front of you, what's around you, and any obstacles.

- **Observe your internal environment.** Listen to the internal dialogue and stories you tell your family and friends, like "I can't hit the podium this year," which can reflect or shape your mental state. Notice sensations and thoughts, but don't judge or try to change them, or take that emotion with you into your training session or competition.

- **Awareness begets awareness.** A side effect of being more mindful while training and competing is you become aware of not only pleasant sensations but also unpleasant ones. Instead of ignoring physical discomfort, rest your attention with the feelings.

- **Practice gratitude.** Be grateful for the team or coaches around you, family, and friends who have supported you and trained with you, as well as yourself for showing up to your training and competition with an open mind and heart. Extend that gratitude to the people involved in keeping the facilities you use in working order and providing the nourishing food that fuels you for movement.

Move: Mindful Walk

• • • • • • • • • • • • •

Many of us walk with the sole purpose of getting from one place to another; we often tell our children to hurry up, over and over again. Young children are experts in the slow walk, stopping to smell the roses, point at ants, pick up rocks to put in their pocket. This mindful activity encourages us to slow things down on a walk. After all, there's tremendous richness of experience to become aware of as we walk, if we awaken to it.

A formal walking meditation can be just as profound as a sitting meditation and has the advantage of bringing the meditative experience into an activity that we often do mindlessly. The act of lifting and dropping each foot to the earth as we move through space was a milestone for you as a young child, something you took great effort to master. There are a number of different walking meditations, all of which empower your feet with the energy of mindfulness. This simple version involves alternating steps with the left and right foot, which helps create a meditative state. Embrace the slower pace as a family walk for an informal mindfulness activity, or engage in a formal mindful walking meditation alone or with your partner.

Age Range: Teens and adults

Directions

- **Where and when.** This meditation is best done outdoors but can be done in the comfort of your home or even in your office. Set aside at least twenty minutes for your walking meditation. Let this be a walk just for meditation (not for errands), so you can sink into the experience with your undivided attention.

- **Start by mindfully standing.** Stand tall, with a soft front and strong back (not stiff). Distribute your weight evenly between your feet. Arms by your sides. Spend a couple of minutes standing still. Notice how your body feels as you are standing. Notice any thoughts or emotions, and let them be.

- **Breathe.** Take some deep breaths, inhaling into the belly. Put your full attention on the sensation of breathing. Allow the breath to return to normal, and notice the natural breathing pattern that develops.

- **Join hands.** Curl the thumb of your left hand in and wrap your fingers around it (like a fist but with your thumb tucked inside). Wrap your right hand around your left hand. Rest your right thumb in the space between your left thumb and index finger. Hold your hands in front of your belly button. The intention here is to reduce the distraction of swinging arms while in your walking meditation.

- **Begin walking.** Slowly shift your weight to the left leg and begin to lift your right foot up. Move it forward and place it back down on the ground. Mindfully shift your weight to the right leg and begin to lift your left foot up, move it forward, and place it back down on the ground. Continue walking at a relaxed, slow pace.

- **Soften your gaze.** Allow your eyes to focus softly ahead of you, taking in the periphery. It's natural to find your attention drawn to the sights around you as you walk, but keep bringing your attention to what is going on internally.

- **Notice how the soles of your feet feel.** Bring your awareness to the contact the soles of your feet make with your socks or shoes, the textures of the fabrics touching them, the way they feel as they bear your body weight. Notice how the entire foot feels as the heel is placed on the ground, and as the movement rolls to the ball of the foot and toes. Notice how it feels as the foot lifts and moves forward. You can reflect on the words of Thich Nhat Hanh as you bring awareness to your feet: "Walk as if you kiss the earth with your feet."

- **Keep breathing.** As you walk, breathe naturally and fully, taking deep breaths. Generally, we have shorter inhales and longer exhales. When you start a walking meditation, begin with two steps on your inhale, three steps on your exhale. Find your rhythm. With regular practice, you will begin to listen to your lungs, and perhaps your breathing pattern becomes three steps on inhale, four or five steps on exhale. If you feel you must take one more step on your inhale, then enjoy one more step on your inhale. Your only job is to enjoy your breath and each step.

- **Mindful turn.** When it's time to turn, whether outdoors or in a room or hallway, do so mindfully. Bring your awareness to the intricate process of turning by noticing every movement required for turning.

- **Half-smile.** You may recall the half-smile practice earlier. Your half-smile can bring on a sense of calm and delight as you move step by step.

- **Body scan.** The entire body is involved in the act of walking, from alternation of the left and right foot to the swinging of your arms and hips. Notice the body sensations of walking with a body scan. Choose whether you'd like to systematically scan your whole body from the soles of your feet upwards to the top of your head, or scan your body randomly, moving your awareness from place to place in your body.

- **Notice a wandering mind.** If your mind starts getting caught up in thoughts, easily bring your attention back to the experience of walking. When your mind goes into planning or rehearsal mode, bring it back by simply focusing on the sensations in your body.

- **Adjust to your terrain.** When you walk up- or downhill, the number of steps per breath will change. Be sure to follow the needs of your lungs, and adjust your breathing pace.

- **Conscious end to the walking meditation.** When the time comes to end the practice, allow yourself to come to a gentle halt. As you find stillness, once again experience yourself standing still. Take a few deep breaths before slowly and mindfully returning to your regular activity.

Upgrade: You can also try heightening your awareness of the rhythm of your walking: the alternation of left and right foot. Simply notice the experience of left-right-left-right motion. There is also an option of bringing counting into this practice, counting steps up from 1 to 10, then coming back to 1 each time you reach 10. Do remember to keep bringing your awareness back to this experience when the mind wanders in thoughts or distractions of the environment.

Explore: Learn more about mindful walking tradition by reading any of Thich Nhat Hanh's books. He is a Zen teacher who has led silent walking meditations with thousands of people at a time. Visit www.plumvillage.org to learn about his village in France, or search online distributors for his books.

Move: Mindful Family Hike

• • • • • • • • • • • • • • • • •

Short, simple mindfulness exercises incorporated into an activity such as hiking are an enjoyable and effective way of being more mindful, solo or with your family. Mindful hiking will soothe your senses and is an ideal opportunity for those who want to experience grounding in nature with their kids. It's a time when you and your children can intentionally stop and smell the wild roses (or eucalyptus). Taking young kids on a trail is not always an easy feat, but I assure you there will be sparks of joy along the way. Knowing the research-backed benefits of being outdoors also helps rationalize the activity for yourself or your partner.

Benefiting from Getting Outdoors

These are just a few benefits of time in nature:

- increases well-being
- helps alleviate stress and anxiety
- promotes creativity
- assists with recovery from mental fatigue
- helps restore attention, boosts the brain's ability to think
- engages the senses

Nourishing Snacks and Family Necessities to Pack

- **Water.** This seems obvious, but it's easy to forget. My eldest started wearing a water pack on his back at age four, but not all kids are into this. If not, it's on you, Mama and Papa, to pack.

- **Fresh fruit.** Choose ones that can survive in a backpack relatively unscathed, like apples or oranges.

- **Bagelwich.** If you are going to pack a sandwich, bagels are heartier than sliced bread and won't get squashed like a sandwich. You can find allergen-friendly bagels like gluten-free or sourdough in fresh baked goods or freezer sections of most grocery stores. I usually opt for the crowd-pleasing cream cheese or PB&J, which stand up to heat.

- **Homemade trail mix.** Go for a fun variety of nuts, seeds, fruit, and more for an adventure with every bite. There are thousands of combinations for all ages and palates. (Check out trail mix recipes on pages 200-201.)

- **Pepperoni or jerky.** If possible, opt for grass-fed, locally sourced meat.

- **Energy balls.** Packed with fat, protein, and carbs, sources of energy for all ages. Explore recipes on pp. x–x.

- **Smoothies.** Seems like an odd addition to this list, but it's a great way to stay hydrated, add an icy ingredient to your bag to keep things cool, and pack in the nutrients. Store in a well-sealed mason jar that can take the bumps on the trek. (Smoothie inspiration on pp. X–X.)

- **Veggie sticks.** Carrots, peppers, celery, and other veggies cut into sticks are great for munching on the trail or at the summit.

- **Facecloths.** You don't eat these, but they are invaluable. Bring dry cloths; wet with the water you've hopefully packed to wipe hands and faces.

- **Sunscreen and bug repellent.** Opt for natural bug repellent and toxin-free sunscreen. Always check labels before using on young children.

- **Reusable bag.** This is great for packing garbage in to take out of your hike, as well as for use if you're going to try making a nature mandala. (Nature mandala instructions on pages 131-133.)

- **Odds and ends.** Noise bells for shoes. Bear spray when warranted or required. First aid kit (or at least Band-Aids).

Tot Trail Notes

One note: don't be in a rush to get in the miles (or less than one mile, which may be covered by your littles). Let me give you a perfect of a recent family hike: my two-year-old stopped on every large rock and tree stump she could climb atop to do a magic show with her magic wand (read: branch). Every. Single. One. But we had no expectations; we don't get a lot of adventure time together, so we just wanted to be outside to soak up fresh air and each other. So for those of you with young kids, here are some top tips I am eager to share:

- **Do a dry run.** It's a good idea to try a hike out without your children before having them join for the trek. Not always possible, but it's something to consider so you see what the terrain is like, get an idea of how long it may take, know if there are restrooms at the trailhead, and so forth.

- **Get to know your neighbors.** The fun of prepping for a hike with little ones begins before you hit the trailhead, as you'll notice from these pointers. Hiking around the block offers a rich learning opportunity for all ages. Parents, learn to identify some local plants or flowers or trees. Learn the call of a bird common to the area.

- **Don't plan for a sweat sesh.** Trails with tots sometimes involve a lot more time spent standing than moving, so have realistic expectations for both yourself and your children. Repeat after me: you're not going with the expectation of getting a workout in.

- **Go early.** Each child is different, but choose a time to start your hike according to when your child's batteries are fully charged. We usually hit trailheads by around 9 a.m.

- **Sightseeing stopovers.** Kids tire easily, and parents may tire mentally quite easily on the trails. On your dry run or when reading up on the family hike you're choosing to do, choose spots such as waterfalls, lookout points, lakes, interpretive centers, and more to stop for rest or refueling.

Mindful Hiking 101

A mindful hike calls for you to immerse yourself in your surroundings by consciously engaging your senses and coming into the present moment, whether that sees you on a neighborhood trail or the Inca Trail. Your body will start to relax, and your mind will begin to settle. Below are instructions for tapping into your senses that you can pick and choose to follow on your own and instruct your children with in language they'll understand:

Look

- Consciously engage your sense of sight.
- Start by turning around slowly and deliberately, taking in the 360-degree view as you do.
- Look up—explore the sky, the patterns in the clouds, the canopy of trees above.
- Look down—notice shadows, patterns, colors, and textures on the ground.
- Sit or lie down for a moment to absorb your surroundings.
- Now look closely at an object that catches your attention, such as a leaf or the bark on a tree. Allow your gaze to soften as you explore the object. Gently observe its colors, shape, and texture. Allow yourself to become really curious about what you're looking at.
- Throughout your hike, try taking snapshots with your mind. When you notice an object or view that you are particularly drawn to or you notice your child is, study it for a few moments

and imprint it on your mind. As you walk on, play it over in your memory for a minute. This is a way to replay the highlights of your hike that you can draw on later in great detail.

Listen

- Consciously engage your sense of listening.
- Close or lower your eyes, keeping your gaze soft.
- Tune into the sounds around you, from the sound of the wind in the trees, to songs of birds, to voices of other hikers.
- Notice if your mind wanders to other senses for anywhere but the act of listening. This is normal. Simply notice where your mind wanders to and gently guide your attention back to the experience of listening.
- If you're hiking solo, with older children, with a partner or friends, you may want to savor a bit of silence for twenty minutes or the duration of the hike. Parents have very few opportunities to experience silence. When it comes to shared silence, note that it can feel a little uncomfortable at first, but there is something magical about it. You can spend the period of silent hiking consciously holding awareness in your body or focus on the sights, sounds, and smells around you.

Touch

- Tune into the sensation of the sun or breeze against your skin.
- If you notice an object with an interesting texture—a rock, soft moss, gnarly root—explore it with your hands, focusing on your sense of touch.
- Bring your awareness down to your feet. Really feel the connection your feet are making with the earth beneath you. Allow yourself to feel grounded, connected, and supported.
- Pay attention to the rise and fall of your chest as you breathe.

Taste

- When you stop to eat your packed lunch or snacks, bring conscious awareness to the taste and texture of your food.

Smell

- Before your hike, pause, close your eyes, and bring conscious awareness to your sense of smell.
- As you're on the trail, periodically take long and slow inhales. Notice the scents dancing in your nose.
- Take pauses throughout your hike to stop, kneel down, and smell the wild roses or other plant life you see along the way.

Move and Play: Mandala Colouring Page

· · · · · · · · · · · · · ·

"The work will wait until you show the child the rainbow, but the rainbow won't wait until the work is done."

—Patricia Clifford

Move and Play: Mindful Running

• • • • • • • • • • • • • • • •

Hit the road solo, run with your partner, or load your kids in the running stroller and head out for a mindful run. No, you won't be running with your eyes shut. A mindful run involves practicing focused awareness exercises while in movement. Start every run by getting a feel for your inner experience at the moment, and then you can choose one or two techniques to bring the practice of mindful awareness while in motion.

Age Range: Teens and adults

Directions

- **Get a feel for what you're feeling.** Do a brief scan of the body from head to toe to pick up any sensations in muscles, joints, and skin. Check in with your emotions. Notice the mental chatter at the moment.

- **Breathe awareness.** As you run, focus on the sensation of your breath.

- **Move.** Keep a strong awareness of everything that's going on around you as you begin your run. Continually bring your attention back to your body. How does it feel now that you're moving?

- **Layers of sound.** As you move along the earth on the route you've chosen, pick up the layers of sound, from your heartbeat, to clothing, to traffic, to nature sounds, to conversations you get a short clip of. Observing the many layers of sound during a run can be helpful if you find that your mind is running wild with thoughts.

- **Toe the line.** Break your run into five segments, one for each toe. For example, for a ten-kilometer run, focus on your little toe for the first two kilometers, the next toe on each foot for the next two-kilometer segment, onward to your big toe for the last two kilometers. When the mind wanders (because it will), just bring it back without judgment to the toe you intended to focus on for the current segment.

- **Use mindful running cues.** You can choose a detailed practice for your next run. You can copy the next page, cut out each individual cue, and pop one in your pocket for the run. Or take a photo and keep as your backdrop on your phone for the run.

I am mindful of . . .

MY BIG TOE TOUCHING DOWN ON THE EARTH & LIFTING OFF OF THE EARTH

I am mindful of . . .

INSTANCES OF JUDGING OR CRITICIZING MYSELF PRE/DURING/POST RUN

I am mindful of . . .

MY BODY ALIGNMENT (CHOOSE 1 AREA TO FOCUS ON: SHOULDERS, CHEST, KNEES, SPINE, HIPS, RIBS…)

I am mindful of . . .

THE RHYTHM OF MY BREATH

I am mindful of . . .

MY HAND POSITIONING

I am mindful of . . .

THOUGHTS PULLING ME INTO THE PAST OR FUTURE, & OUT OF THE PRESENT MOMENT

I am mindful of . . .

THE SCENTS IN THE AIR

I am mindful of . . .

EMOTIONS PULLING ME INTO THE PAST OR FUTURE, & OUT OF THE PRESENT MOMENT

I am mindful of . . .

THE COLOURS AROUND ME

I am mindful of . . .

ANY AREAS OF TENSION IN MY BODY

I am mindful of . . .

SENSATIONS OF THE WIND, SUN & MY RUNNING CLOTHING AGAINST MY SKIN

I am mindful of . . .

THE SOUNDS AROUND ME

Move and Play: Family Yoga

• • • • • • • • • • • • • •

As a kids, teens, and family yoga teacher, as well as a practitioner in my own home (where my son usually leads our time on the mat), I wanted to share some of my learnings and a practice with you and your family.

Age Range: All ages

Directions

- **Set the mood.** Set a huge mood for family yoga practice with music and diffusing oils (check out blends on page 115). Turn off distractions like TVs and phones.

- **Pick a theme.** A fun way to engage younger children in a yoga practice is to bring in playful themes such as "a trip to the zoo" or "barnyard animals" or "superheroes." You then give the yoga poses fitting names that follow the theme. For example, Warrior III could be referred to as Superboy or Supergirl, or an easy pose as Butterfly.

- **Props for practice.** While not necessary, your family may enjoy having props such as pillows, bolsters, and blocks handy during practice. Large hardcover books can be used in place of blocks for sitting, and rolled towels are a good substitute for bolsters.

- **Practice.** To reap the benefits of yoga requires practice. Try working in a regular yoga practice for yourself, you and your partner, or the whole family one to two times per week. Create boundaries to protect the time for this practice, whether it's happening in home or at a studio. If at home, try this fun and engaging family yoga sequence.

Science: Yoga has been found in research to improve mental and physical well-being of all ages, from childhood through adulthood (Chong et al. 2011; Hagen and Nayar 2014; Ross et al. 2013). For younger populations in particular, yoga can improve resilience, mood, and self-regulation skills pertaining to emotions and stress (Hagen and Nayar 2014; Ross Thomas 2010).

easy

table

cat

cow

sunbird

child

plank

cobra

downward dog

half downward dog

standing forward bend

high lunge

warrior II

triangle

warrior III

mountain

standing forward bend

yoga squat

camel

child

dead bug

happy baby.

savasana

easy

Move and Play: Partner Yoga

• • • • • • • • • • • • • • • •

Practicing yoga with another person, whether a partner, child, or friend, is an excellent way for two people to relate to one another through assisted poses. Partner yoga poses can add resistance, and you can try new poses or find deeper expressions of familiar poses. Doing yoga together is an activity that is fun and playful, as well as a way to connect and test your ability to trust each other. Some poses are easier when partners are similar height, but most are accessible no matter your size.

Age Range: All ages

Directions

- **Choose a yoga sequence.** Choose a yoga sequence (like the family yoga practice on pages 99-100). You can also choose to watch a guided class online.

- **Infuse or end your practice with partner poses.** Most guided yoga classes you'll find online won't include partner poses. And the family yoga sequence on the previous page doesn't include partner poses. So choose to add the poses you like and feel ready to try in your practice where it seems fitting. You may also choose to end your practice connecting with your partner or child in a partner pose or two.

- **Have fun.** Partner poses aren't about pushing yourself or your partner past your edge. Take a playful approach to partner poses and see where they take you (which may include to the ground, and that's okay).

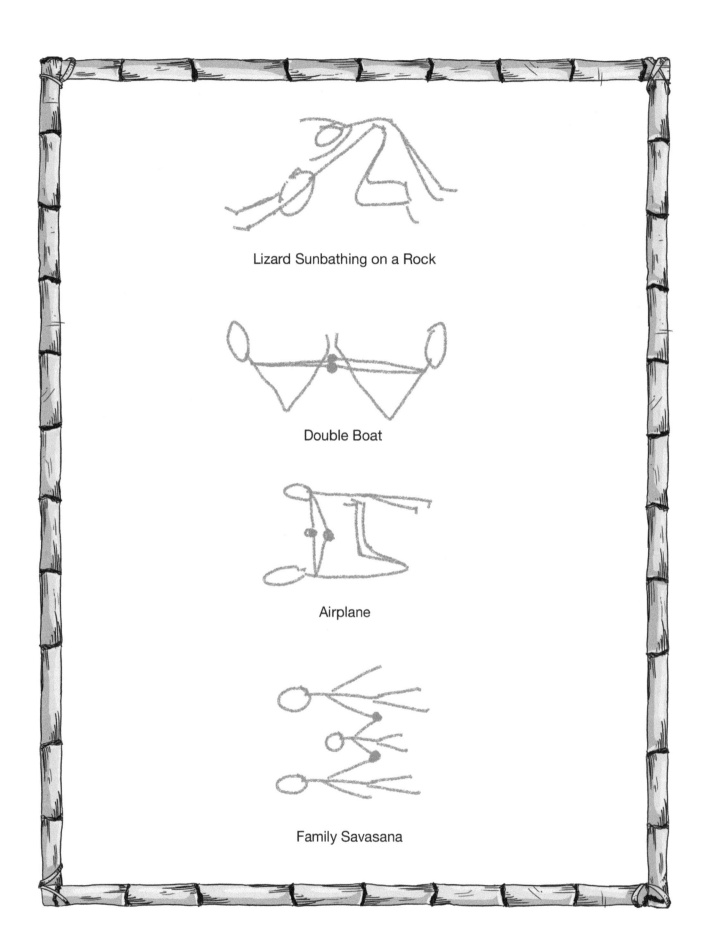

Lizard Sunbathing on a Rock

Double Boat

Airplane

Family Savasana

Move and Play: Six Tips for Being Present with Play

• • • • • • • • • • • • • •

We all have a deep desire to connect with our kids and give them a sense of belonging and acceptance in our families. Being present in play can be a practice to support this. Being present isn't just about giving your children attention (they already have that most of the day). Rather, it's about being intentional about really connecting with them.

Tips for being present in play:

1. **Make the (play) time.** Try carving out thirty minutes daily when you can give undivided attention to your children while taking part in an activity of their choosing.

2. **Set an intention.** You've worked on setting a mindful parenting intention in this book. Try reflecting on it before or during play. You can also just mentally repeat the mantra "play present" that you say as your mind wanders to other activities you could be doing (which are usually less fun, chores).

3. **Reduce tech distractions.** TVs and phones are two of the biggest distractions in family life. At the very least, turn TVs of, set your ringer to silent, and put your phone more than arm's length away (or even in the tech bed for a nap).

4. **Mind your mind, then your hands**. When you start to feel your mind racing with tasks (because that's what adult minds are wired to do), notice where your mind has gone, then direct your attention to your hands and whatever it is they are doing in the play.

5. **Don't judge yourself.** Kids like to repeatedly do the same tasks or games, and for adults, this can get boring. It's okay to feel this way, and there's no need to feel guilty or judge yourself as a bad parent. Just come back to your intention of doing child-led play for the time you've set aside. Society sends us mixed messages about how much time we should spend playing with children. Too much time, and some say you are letting your child ruin your life. Too little time, you may spur a feeling of guilt for taking time to yourself. Find your own balance, and let go of guilt from within or around you.

6. **Practice gratitude.** Wow, you have thirty minutes uninterrupted to hang out with your child to play? And with a plethora of choices for toys? Pretty lucky. Why not share these grateful sentiments aloud during or after play, and ask your child what they're grateful for from the play time with Mama or Papa. Their answer will likely be rewarding for you as a parent and motivate you to continue the play time in the daily routine.

Science: Researchers have shown that relationships with family is an important source of happiness. Play is a way to connect and experience joy.

be present in play

Move and Play: Emotions Charades

• • • • • • • • • • • • • •

What better way to teach your children about feelings than through play? This activity will help your children expand their emotional intelligence to support them in identifying different emotions that their parents, siblings, classmates, and others express.

Understanding how another person may be feeling in a given situation helps children respond thoughtfully. Acting out emotions and behavioral responses in a safe environment gives them the tools they need to handle big emotions when they arise. The basic gist is that instead of using movie titles, animals, places, or other words, you use emotions.

Age Range: 5+

Materials

- Feelings words, with optional pictures on sheets of paper (see worksheet)

- Bowl

Directions

- **Choose the feelings for the game.** You can write down feeling words on a sheet of paper or print out the worksheet found on the next page. Cut out the individual emotions and put them in a bowl. You could substitute written words for pictures showing the emotion.

- **Make teams or play individually.** The family can split into two teams and have teammates guess the feelings for points, or a parent and child can play together trying to guess each other's feelings.

- **Take turns.** Flip a coin to choose who will be the first performer. Take turns picking a slip of paper from the bowl and acting out that emotion without saying anything out loud.

- **Guess the emotion.** Depending if you are playing singles or team, your opposing player or your teammates guess the emotion you are acting out.

- **Track the play.** You can keep track of team points on a piece of paper or board.

- **Reflect on the experience.** After the game, reflect on it. Here are some questions you can ask:

  - "What cues did I use to guess what another person was feeling?"

  - "If it was easy at times, what helped make it easy?"

- "If it was challenging, what made it challenging to figure out the feeling?"

- "How do our feelings affect people around us?"

- **Have a real-life talk.** Help your children realize that outside of this game, it can be difficult to know what another person is feeling. This is especially true when we don't know the other person well, or when the other person is feeling multiple feelings at one time. Encourage your child not to jump to any conclusions about someone else's feelings. Explain how we can watch for clues to guide our guesses like we did in the game, but the *best* way to know and understand another person's feelings is to ask him or her. Next, we communicate support and understanding.

- **Define empathy.** Take this as a teaching moment to explain that understanding how another person is feeling is called empathy, and when we express empathy toward others, it shows we care about them.

Upgrade: For older children, you can have a discussion about how emotions and feelings aren't the same thing. While emotions are associated with bodily reactions that are activated through neurotransmitters released by the brain, feelings play out in our minds only.

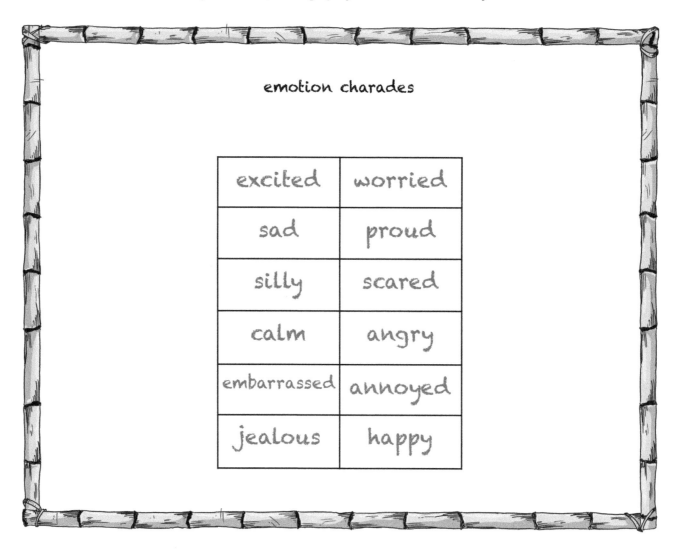

emotion charades

excited	worried
sad	proud
silly	scared
calm	angry
embarrassed	annoyed
jealous	happy

Move and Play: The Mindful Mamas and Papas Play Date

Looking for a fun take on a night in or out with friends and to bring your attention to meaningful social connections? If you said yes (Oh, please say you said yes), check out these ideas for parents' play dates because play dates aren't just for kids. Taking time away from your family can be both mentally and physically challenging. But social support, connection, physical fitness, and self-care make us better moms and dads. These factors can aid you in breezing through some of those challenging days.

Upgrade: Hint: it can also be helpful to get those phones away to avoid technoference in your closest relationships.

Popcorn and a Movie

Mamas, get your girls together for a movie date. You'll just need popcorn, topped with coconut oil or butter and salt. If you want to pair with wine, go for a buttery chardonnay. Get a good movie on. Perhaps a stand-up comedy show, a series on Netflix from your late teens/early twenties, a wine-themed movie like *Sideways* or *SOMM*, or a PVR of your favorite reality TV show. Serve popcorn and wine in mason jars if you don't have all the same types of bowls or enough wine glasses, and it's such a quaint serving vessel.

Baking Date

While you may be conditioned to have milk with your cookies, turns out particular cookies pair amazingly with particular wine. So make a date around this; encourage friends to each pick a cookie recipe and ingredients needed for their chosen recipe, get together, and do some baking (and sipping). Have some store-bought or homemade cookies and a bottle of wine ready for when you welcome your friends. Don't get just any wine; be mindful of your choices of wine. Just as you look into whether the food you consume is organic, you should be mindful of your wine source too. I adore biodynamic, organic, as well as Old World wines (these tend not to have pesticides and additives).

Take a bite and sip of these pairs:

- chocolate chip cookies to pair with cabernet sauvignon or Syrah or Shiraz

- oatmeal raisin cookies to pair with a pinot noir

- ginger snaps (see recipe for raw ginger snaps on page 206) to pair with a zinfandel

- shortbread cookies with chardonnay

Sweat Date

Sometimes it's hard to balance our schedule to fit in fitness and friend time. Easy solution: the sweat date. It's a pretty simple formula: movement and sharing food or drink as fitting focal points for connecting with friends. You can do what you normally do, just with company. Or try something new or introduce a friend to a new activity. Here are some ideas:

- **Yin and vin.** Head to a yin yoga class (even better if you have a local studio with a candlelight yin class). Follow it up with a glass of wine at a spot you can walk to from the studio.

- **Flow and matcha.** Hit up a faster paced flow yoga class and head to a local coffee or tea house that serves matcha tea. Matcha gives a kick of energy that for some should be reserved to consuming earlier in the day, as opposed to the evening.

- **Barre and brunch.** I know my mama friends would love a chance for weekend brunch. However, with toddlers, brunch is seldom restful. Have your brunch and eat it too by planning a barre class with one or more friends, followed by a brunch that will satisfy your group's taste buds.

- **Mindful run/hike and picnic.** Meet a friend at a spot, near a parked car, at the office, or at home, where you can store a picnic while you adventure. Each plan to bring a simple dish to snack on (such as veggies and hummus, chia pudding from page 174, smoothies in mason jars on pages 166-171). Go for a hike or run free of tech so you can be fully in each other's presence. Then find stillness as you carry your mindful awareness onto the picnic blanket as you share food and conversation with each other.

Create

Create: Introduction

• • • • • • • • • • • • • •

These days, everyone loves DIY activities: kids, teens, and parents too. Pinterest and various online sites are rife with ideas, but it's hard deciphering which ones are good and which are destined for a #pinterestfail. Flip through this section and try any of these activities of varying levels of difficulty. Many of the crafts involve reducing toxins in the home, recycling goods, and using materials from nature.

Create: The Get-to-Do List

• • • • • • • • • • • • • • • •

To-do lists: They come between parents. They come between your intentions as a parent and the experience of being bogged down by a list of shoulds. Or perhaps you are carrying all the tasks of the day, week, year, from appointments to grocery lists, in your head or spread across multiple apps on your phone, leaving you in a state of disarray and disorganization. There is no getting past the fact you as a parent have activities and appointments and shopping to attend to. But having a full life is a gift. Let's try to reframe your typical to-do list by infusing positivity and viewing it as a get-to-do list you get to create, mamas and papas. This is a way of infusing positivity into the tasks on your plate. You can get additional copies of this to-do list on the book website.

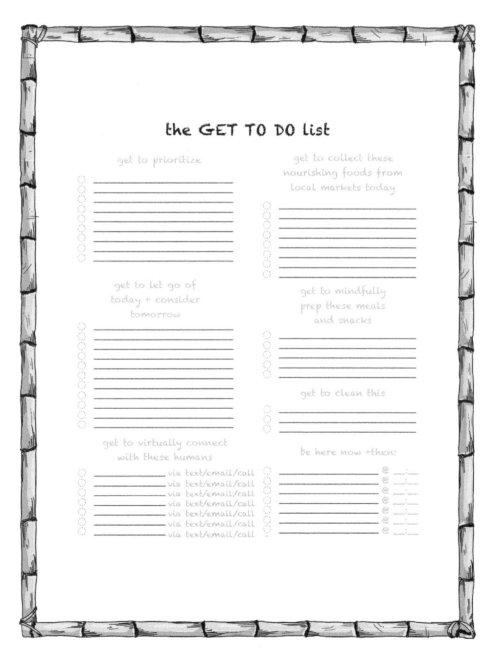

Create: Mindful Space Creation

• • • • • • • • • • • • • •

Mindfulness doesn't just happen. It takes intention setting and practice. Part of the practice is curating a space suited to your family's needs, a place where you can use the tools and practice the exercises included in this book. Create a mindful space that inspires and grounds your family today.

Age Range: Parents, with optional assistance of children

Directions

- **Set an intention.** Close your eyes and think about your intention for creating a mindful space. Maybe it's to serve as an area to support your children in learning skills for self-regulation, or to inspire you creatively, or to heal. The most common reason is simply to create a space that reflects back the energy of your and your family's meditation practice.

- **Find time.** What time of day will work best for you as a parent for at-home exercises? Tell others who need to know that you're no available at this time. Make an effort to protect your time for mindfulness practice, length of time, and anything else you would like to track. Do this same step, bringing intention to dedicating time for your child's mindful movement of the day.

- **Find space.** Where will your dedicated mindfulness practice space be? Ideally, somewhere quiet and private. Make it a comfortable space by having cushions and blankets and an audio device to play any mindfulness tracks you choose. It could just be a corner of your dresser, a bedside table, or a corner in the garden. Once you choose a spot, consider placing a yoga mat, yoga block, pillow, large rock, tree stump, or stool in front of it to delineate the space.

- **Collect.** Place objects in your and your child's mindful space that have special significance or meaning for you and that tap into the five senses. Consider touch (jewelry such as a mala necklace), sight (photographs, statues of deities, lights, candles, prints of meaningful quotes), smell (fresh or dried flowers, candles, essential oil diffuser), and taste (tea, food, water). You may also want to add something from your adventures in nature that taps into numerous senses, from flowers to rocks to driftwood and more. Some refer to these areas as altars, but don't feel as if this requires a Buddha figurine or the like. Be true to yourself and your beliefs. There are no rules or must-have pieces for an altar; just choose something you can direct your own devotion toward.

- **Journal.** Consider having a journal and pen in your mindful space to make notes about your family's mindfulness practice. Perhaps even just a word or two to describe the day's practice ("wandering mind" or "present" or "energizing"), thinking patterns, type of meditation you practiced.

- **Change it up.** Your intention may evolve day to day, or week to week. Likewise, so can your mindful space. Swap out pictures, replace dried flowers with fresh ones, add pieces as they come into your life.

- **Mindfulness on the go.** If you're a frequent traveler, have smaller versions of some of your altar items (family photos, small charms), or bring one piece from your altar with you, and perhaps download meditation tracks or a meditation app like Calm or Headspace or Insight Timer.

- **Kitchen altar.** In your own kitchen, you might want to create an altar similar to the one you create for your mindful space. The intention of a kitchen altar is to be a reminder to practice mindfulness while meal planning, cooking, eating, and cleaning up. It may just be a small shelf with enough room for a candle or incense holder or diffuser. Perhaps even a small flower vase or terrarium or herb plant. You could also have a beautiful stone, a small picture: whatever is meaningful to you. When you come into the kitchen, you can begin your work by offering scent into the air with your candle/incense/oils, practicing breathing, and making the kitchen into a meditation hall.

- **Create a mindful space with your children.** Mindful spaces aren't just for adults. Serving as a guide for your child, walk through the above steps together. Choose an area in the home or backyard that will be your child's mindful space. Make it welcoming with their own mat, chair, or pillow. Encourage them to bring a few objects that have special meaning to them, such as a family photo, their favorite artwork, or a remnant of the earth such as a twig, stone, or plant.

Create: Essential Crafting Body Buddha

• • • • • • • • • • • • • • • •

Mamas and Papas, self-care isn't selfish, so slather it on. And give the gift of massage to your kids. Tap into your senses as you prepare this homemade self-care tool that you can put your own personal stamp on. This is a nontoxic body butter that can be used for all ages, with or without the addition of essential oils; it has scientifically proven benefits for skin health.

Age Range: All ages, with parent supervision to heat and prepare

Materials

- 1 small mason jar (or recycled jam or salsa jar)
- ½ cup shea butter
- ¼ cup olive, grape seed, almond, avocado, or jojoba oil
- 10–20 drops essential oil (optional; check out blending options on page 115)

Directions

- Scoop shea butter into a mason jar. You can buy cases wholesale or reuse old jam jars
- Put in a pot with boiling water.
- Stir the shea butter until fully melted.
- Remove from heat and stir in preferred vegetable oil and essential oils.
- Cool in fridge.
- Once solid, store anywhere (purse, gym bag, swim bag, bathroom, bedside table, kitchen).
- To soothe skin or for mornings when you need a refreshing boost, apply chilled cream to face or body.

Science: Plant oils have been utilized for a variety of purposes throughout history, with their integration into foods and skin care products. Various plant oils have been found to act as a protective barrier to the skin, allow skin to retain moisture, have antimicrobial and anti-inflammatory properties, and promote wound healing. Fixed oils, such as shea butter, serve as a carrier to distribute on the skin essential oils that have their own unique health benefits, depending on the chosen oils or blends of essential oils. In the Body Buddha recipe, we highlight shea butter, which comes from the kernels of the fruit of the shea tree. Shea butter has been extensively studied and found to possess potent anti-inflammatory and antioxidant properties (Maryann and Wiesman 2004), as well as boost collagen production and demonstrate antiaging properties (Oluwaseyi Israel 2014).

Upgrade: Looking for a baby shower gift, holiday present, or just a sweet little something for a friend? Make a jar, cut a square of fabric, place fabric over lid, secure with elastic, then tie a bow and add a note to the special recipient.

Note: Consult with health care professional before using essential oils for yourself and your children.

Create: Essential Crafting Blends

• • • • • • • • • • • • • •

Check out these essential oil blends for the office, kitchen, mama and papa's room, kids' rooms, study areas, and special events.

Age Range: Adults

Materials: Your preferred essential oils

- Mindful Papa: 2 white fir and 2 cypress and 2 wintergreen
- Mindful Mama: 2 arborvitae and 2 bergamot and 2 orange
- Mindful Mini: 1 drop each lavender and orange
- Calming: 1 drop each of bergamot and lavender and patchouli and ylang-ylang
- Grounding: 2 chamomile and 3 sandalwood and 3 vetiver
- Good Morning: 2 peppermint and 2 orange
- Dinner Party: 2 lavender and 2 lemon and 2 rosemary
- Oatmeal Cookies: 2 cedarwood and 2 cassia or cinnamon and 3 orange
- Clean Laundry: 3 white fir and 3 cypress and 2 wintergreen
- Fresh and Clean: 2 drops each of lavender and lemon and rosemary
- Study Time: 2 drops each rosemary and peppermint
- Spa Vibe: 2 lavender and 2 lemon and 2 peppermint
- Hawaiian Getaway: 3 orange and 2 sandalwood and 3 grapefruit
- Yoga Studio: 4 lime and 3 grapefruit and 2 clary sage
- Staycation: 3 bergamot and 2 frankincense
- Spring: 1 clary sage and 1 geranium and 1 lavender and 1 chamomile
- Summer: 1 patchouli and 2 bergamot and 3 orange
- Fall: 3 orange and 1 ginger and 1 clove and 1 frankincense
- Winter: 2 cinnamon and 2 white fir

Directions

- **Diffuse.** Place essential oils in a diffuser where you desire a scent-ual experience.
- **Bath salts.** Make your own bath salt blends. Simply get a glass jar or Tupperware tub and mix 2 cups of Epsom salts and ½ cup baking soda and 30 drops total of essential oils. Depending on the size of your tub, use ¼ to ½ cup of your salt blend per mindful bath experience. Store in dry, cool place.
- **Pure-fume.** Make nontoxic perfumes from pure essential oils and vegetable oil. Just add 10–20 drops of essential oil (choose your own or portion out based on recipes above) to a 5 milliliter roller bottle. Fill the rest of the bottle with vegetable oil of your choosing (such as fractionated coconut oil, sweet almond oil, jojoba oil). Stop the roller ball to the bottle. Shake to combine ingredients. Roll onto your wrists, on your neck, or behind your ears.

Note: Please consult with health care professional before using diffusers and perfume rollers with pregnant women and children.

Create: Aroma-Dough

● ● ● ● ● ● ● ● ● ● ● ● ● ● ● ● ●

No need to buy the neon dough when you can literally whip up this sensory and scents-y craft on the stovetop with ease and for pennies. This is a recipe for a nontoxic playdough that can be used by young kids to raise sensory awareness and build motor skills, or teens and mamas and papas to relieve stress by using as stress balls.

Age Range: 3+

Materials

- 1 cup all-purpose flour
- ½ cup salt
- 2 tsp cream of tartar
- 1 cup water or cooled tea
- 1½ Tbsp olive oil
- Nontoxic food coloring (store-bought or homemade)
- Scent (5 drops of essential oil, tea in place of water, or spices such as cinnamon and cloves)

Directions

- In medium saucepan, mix together all ingredients except scents and colors.
- Heat mixture over medium heat, stirring constantly.
- Eventually, you will produce a ball of dough.
- Let dough cool.
- Add essential oils, spices, and color.
- Play time with the aroma-do.
- Store in a sealed container. These may be repurposed old dough containers, glass baby food containers, or mason jars.

Upgrade: Did you know you can use foods in your pantry or fridge to make your own food coloring for baking, cooking, and crafting? Go to your web browser to check out blog posts and video tutorials on how to prep DIY food coloring. Here are some color sources:

- pink: strawberries, raspberries
- red: beets, tomato
- orange: carrots, paprika
- yellow: saffron, turmeric
- green: matcha, spirulina, spinach
- blue: red cabbage and baking soda
- purple: blueberries
- brown: coffee, tea, cocoa
- black: activated charcoal

Science: These are some benefits of crafting your own aroma-do at home:

Fine Motor Development

The malleable properties of playdough makes it fun for investigation and exploration. It aids in building up strength in all the tiny hand muscles and tendons, prepping them for pencil and scissor control later on. As part of simple and tactile play, it can be squashed, squeezed, rolled, flattened, chopped, cut, raked, poked, or shredded. Each one of these different actions aids fine motor development in a different way, not to mention hand-eye coordination and general concentration.

Imagination and Creativity

Introducing open-ended play items to playdough makes it a great medium for numerous types of imaginative play and can represent so many things in a kid's eyes.

Calming and Soothing

Little kids often struggle to express their emotions. Using playdough while talking and singing can help with that process. Essential oils can help with this, as well (see below).

Math and Literacy Development

Kids can form letters of the alphabet, spell their name, make numbers, form 2-D and 3-D shapes, compare lengths/thicknesses/weights, match and sort by color, and much more.

Science and Discovery

The act of making the playdough together lets kids practice measuring, explore, and observe the changing state of materials in a hands-on way.

Essential Oils

Essential oils are great tools for the home. Here are a few favorites:

- lavender (relaxing, calmative; Mama and Papa's little helper in transitioning from playtime into nap time).

- bergamot (unique citrus oil with ability to be both uplifting and calming)

- peppermint (can boost concentration, alertness, focus, and memory)

Create: Mindful Coloring

• • • • • • • • • • • • •

Adult coloring books are no longer just found in an art therapist's office; they now are found in stacks at big box warehouses. If you're looking for an activity to help chill out, this is for you and your kids.

Age Range: 10+

Materials

• Sharpened pencil crayons

Directions

• Choose one page featuring a food item or mandala to color.

• If your mind wanders, notice where it goes and come back to the sensation of the pencil crayon in your hand and the image before your eyes.

• If you so choose, you can display your work of mindful art on a fridge, in a frame in your mindful space, or at your place of work.

• You can use a colored mandala in a frame as a focal point for a focusing meditation.

Science: Coloring has therapeutic potential to reduce anxiety and bring about mindfulness. The act of coloring for all ages allows one to switch off other thoughts and focus, similar to the practice of meditation. A 2005 research study proved anxiety levels dropped when subjects colored mandalas, which are round frames with geometric patterns inside (see examples on the following pages).

Food is Joy

Create: Mala Making

· · · · · · · · · · · · · · · · · ·

You've likely seen this physical symbol of spirituality worn proudly around wrists and necks. The mala is an ancient spiritual tool that's been used for thousands of years to keep count of mantras during a meditation. The mala is a physical reminder of your mindful mama and papa intention. Wear your intention, and let it be a gentle reminder to support you.

Mala Beads

A traditional mala necklace has 108 beads. You can make a shorter mala by using factors of 108 (18, 27, 36, 54). There are many reasons why 108 is significant. Among them: it's said there are 108 energy lines that converge to form the heart chakra; the diameter of the sun is 108 times the diameter of the earth. The guru bead is a bead larger than the rest of the beads on the mala creation; it represents your teacher in life and the teacher within yourself. It lies outside the circle of 108 beads, above the tassel.

Why Hop on the Bead Bandwagon?

For some, it's a spiritual statement and practice reminder. But the mala is a gift for all ages, regardless of religious affiliation (or lack thereof). A mala can be made for babies, kids, teens, and parents. Nontoxic rubber beads can be used for nursing moms or teething babes (found on Etsy or Amazon). Mala making for kids (beading onto a small string) can be used to raise sensory awareness and build motor skills. Malas are an excellent exercise in focused awareness, both making them and using them. Teens and adults can shop for or collect beads and charms to create a custom work of art that can be used for repetition of mantras or intentions, to count breaths to calm the nervous system, or to engage in breath work premeditation.

Make Your Own Mala

Sure, you could purchase a mala necklace or bracelet, but why not make it a personal work of art you wear to remind you of your intention for mindful living? You can do this craft as a solo, partner, or family activity. Or have it at the center of a gathering of your parent friends or a sleepover or birthday party for your kids.

Age Range: 5+

Materials

- Beads (you can go for traditional 108, or do a factor of 108: 18, 27, 36, 54)
- Spacer beads (these small beads are optional for younger children; saves doing the spacer knots for those working on building motor skills)

- 1 mm waxed cotton or hemp cord (five feet long for necklace, less for bracelet)
- 1 guru bead (large bead or charm)
- 1 tassel (silk, cotton, horsehair)
- Scissors
- Clear nail polish to coat ends of string
- Essential oil (optional, added to beads that can absorb oil)

Directions

- **Set an intention**. Before you begin, give thought to what meaning you want for your mala.

- **Bracelet or necklace?** Choose if you're going to do a necklace or bracelet. Cut string accordingly.

- **Cut the cord accordingly.** After you cut the cord, use clear nail polish to coat a few inches of one end of the cord. Allow time for it to dry. This is to make stringing beads easier. Tie off one end of your cord, leaving a seven-inch tail that will be used to tie on the tassel.

- **Start stringing beads.** String your first bead onto the cord.

- **To knot or not to knot.** Make a tight knot against the bead. For an easier route and for younger artists, choose to add small beads roughly the size of a knot between the regular size beads making up your mala.

- **Repeat**. Continue this repetition 18 to 108 times.

- **Tie it up**. When you've finished stringing the beads, tie the two ends together with a knot.

- **Get your guru bead on.** String your guru bead onto both pieces of cord at the bottom of the mala. Tie another knot against the guru bead, using both cords.

- **Tie on the tassel**. Attach the tassel below the guru bead. Tie and secure with knots multiple times. Use the clear nail polish to coat the knots.

- **Add essential oils**. If desired, you can put a couple drops of essential oil onto just the guru bead or throughout the string of beads making up your mala.

Explore: Search online for images or videos of mala bracelets and necklaces to get inspiration.

Upgrade: Once complete, you have a mindfulness tool you can take with you anywhere. Use your mala for mindfulness exercises regularly, whether using single beads for mantra repetition (make your own or check out page 23-27 for mom-tras and man-tras) or full breath cycles (inhale-pause-exhale-pause). This exercise can provide a pause for you to step back and see a situation more clearly. Your frustration, anger, or other emotion you feel stuck in may not feel so overwhelming. You'll feel a greater sense of control. Your attitude to your children may soften. You can become more competent in dealing with their behavior.

Create: Worry Catcher

. . . .

Worries come up for all children, teens, as well as mamas and papas. For some, worries are more frequent. This craft allows you—no matter your age—to send your worries to a worry catcher (or dream catcher) so you don't have to hold onto them anymore. You can find video tutorials online for intricate designs of worry catchers. These directions below are all optional and basic ways to make your first worry catcher:

Age Range: 3–8 with adult help; 9+ unassisted

Materials

- Paper plate or a wood or metal hoop found in yarn or crochet aisles of craft shops
- Scissors
- Yarn
- Tape
- Feathers
- Beads
- Hold puncher
- Markers
- Fabric scraps
- Lace material
- Scrap paper
- Stickers
- Markers
- Crochet doily (if you'd like material for the middle and want to skip the weave pattern with yarn)
- Other trinkets or materials from nature

Directions

- **Choose your core for the worry catcher.** Choose either a paper plate or a metal hoop.

- **Prep your paper plate.** If using a paper plate, cut out the center to just leave a hoop-like shape on which to create your worry catcher design. Ensure you have approximately two inches of edging. Punch holes around the inside edge of the paper plate.

- **Put your creative touch on the plate**. You can color or draw designs or put stickers on the paper plate ring.

- **Start threading**. Roll a piece of tape around the tip of a long piece of yarn to help thread through holes of the worry catcher, and to thread to beads. String yarn through holes bordering the plate or around the hoop.

- **Bring on the beads**. Add beads on the yarn throughout the center or hanging pieces.

- **Create layers or textures.** You can do this by tying knots or braiding pieces together.

- **Feather and fabric your catcher.** Tie knots around bundles of feathers or single feathers to hang from the worry catcher. You can add fabric scraps, lace, or yarn strings to the bottom of the paper plate or hoop.

- **Display.** When the worry catcher is completed, hang it in your child's room or mindful space.

- **Use as a reminder of mindfulness practice.** These are great pieces to hang in bedrooms and throughout the home, including the area designated as a mindful space, and serve as a reminder of mindfulness practice.

Upgrade: Integrate breathing exercises while using the worry catcher (pages 128-129).

Science: While worries are normal in childhood, anxiety disorders affect one in eight children and one in four teens (National Institute of Mental Health 2017). Untreated children with anxiety disorders are at a higher risk of performing poorly in school, miss out on important social experiences, and engage in substance abuse. Be sure to see a health professional if you believe your child experiences a higher than normal level of nervousness, fear, or shyness, or avoids places and activities.

Explore: Visit a video site or search engine, and type in terms such as "DIY tutorial dream catcher" or "paper plate dream catcher" or "worry catcher" to get some inspiration or more detailed instructions for creating a worry catcher.

Create: Smell and Tell

· · · · · · · · · · · · · ·

Tapping into the senses is a gateway for mindful awareness. When it comes to kids, they are so curious: always poking, squishing, prodding, stretching, and smelling things in their environment and on their plates. This exercise draws upon their curious nature.

Age Range: Eighteen months+

Materials

- Choose materials or food with a scent (fresh orange peel, sprig of rosemary, fresh flowers, a cup of dirt).

Directions

- **Gather round.** Whether just as a family around the dinner table, or with a group of friends, pass something fragrant to each child.

- **Pick a scent, any scent.** You can choose the same item for each child or give each child a unique item. Examples include a fresh orange peel, sprig of rosemary, fresh flowers, a cup of dirt.

- **Teach a mindful breath and tapping into the sense of smell.** Prompt children to close their eyes and inhale the scent of the object in their hands, focusing all their attention on the smell of that object.

- **Allow time for silence and investigation.** Scent can be a powerful tool for easing worries, tapping into memories, and anchoring into the present.

- **Keep exploring the sense of smell as a mindful tool.** If children wish, they can then open their eyes and investigate the object by tapping into their other senses, such as sense of sight, tastes, touch, and hearing.

Create: Nature Mandala

• • • • • • • • • • • • • • • •

This mindful craft combines the beauty of the natural world with your family's artistic touch. You get to investigate nature and make a mandala of your own with organic supplies you discover outdoors. You'll use natural elements such as flowers, stones, seeds, twigs, pine cones, shells, and more to create a nature mandala. Making nature mandalas in the sand or dirt is an excellent family activity that isn't a strain to keep one's mindful awareness tapped into, no matter the age. This activity will keep children and parents alike entertained for an hour or more, as you collect all the natural elements to complete a nature mandala. Creating nature mandalas is a mindful activity that promotes relaxation and reduces anxiety, and the resulting work can be used as a focusing tool during meditation.

Age Range: 2+

Materials

- Flowers
- Stones
- Fern leaves
- Twigs
- Seashells
- Seeds
- Dried grass
- Bark
- Driftwood
- Natural materials you or your children have collected on family vacations, such as sea glass, shells, sand, pebbles
- Paper, recycled cardboard, tree trunk, sand, or dirt as the canvas for the nature mandala
- Nontoxic glue

Directions

- **Forage the land for natural elements.** Try not to disturb living plants, but rather choose vegetation such as flower pieces or branches that have fallen to the ground.

- **Choose your canvas.** Decide whether you're going to use paper, cardboard, sand, tree trunk, dirt, sand, or another canvas for your individual or family mandala.

- **Prepare your canvas.** If doing on the ground, clear a circular area to serve as the canvas for your mandala. If doing on paper or cardboard, have glue handy to secure your natural elements to your backdrop.

- **Begin your creation.** Create a circular motif with symmetrical geometry. You can use a stick in the sand or dirt or a pencil or pen on paper to create patterns around your natural elements, as well.

- **Capture the mandala moment.** Take a picture of the finished product to preserve the moment and admire the natural beauty. You can have it as your smart phone or tablet backdrop image to remind you of this zen family moment. Or print the photos to frame or create a mandala photo album that contains all your family's nature mandalas.

- **Close the activity with a mantra.** Guide everyone to capture the image of their mandala with their eyes, imprinting it in their mind, and then instruct them to close their eyes for a moment. Still seeing the mandala in the mind, share a mantra aloud three times. Inhale and say with the exhalation, "I am creative. I am calm. I am happy." Repeat three rounds of deep and slow inhalation, exhalation, mantra.

- **Making a nature mandala keepsake.** If you or your children have made a mandala on a piece of paper or cardboard, allow it to dry. Once dry, you can put it in a frame or in a shadow box to put up in the home or office.

Upgrade: You can use this mandala—whether a photo or a framed nature mandala on cardboard or paper—for a focusing meditation (page 65) or as a decoration for your mindful altar (pages 112-113).

Science: When on a walk through a neighborhood pathway, in the forest, or along the seaside, notice the patterns on shells, flowers, or pine cones.

- Nearly all flowers contain a circular center filled with tiny blooms that form a natural mandala. The outer rings of the flower also form a natural mandala that is typically made up of petals that may be solid colored or may have layers of variegated color.

- Ferns have a spiral of delicate leaves that create a natural mandala.

- Many seashells create a natural mandala with spirals of multicolored shells.

- A variety of fruits and vegetables, like citrus fruits and cucumber, conceal a natural mandala in their center. Citrus fruits like oranges, lemons, and limes have a center with an array of fruit segments. Cucumbers form natural mandalas with the seeds and flesh coming out from the core of the fruit.

- Imagine a circle connecting the six points of a snowflake, and you'll see a mandala made up of tiny ice crystals.

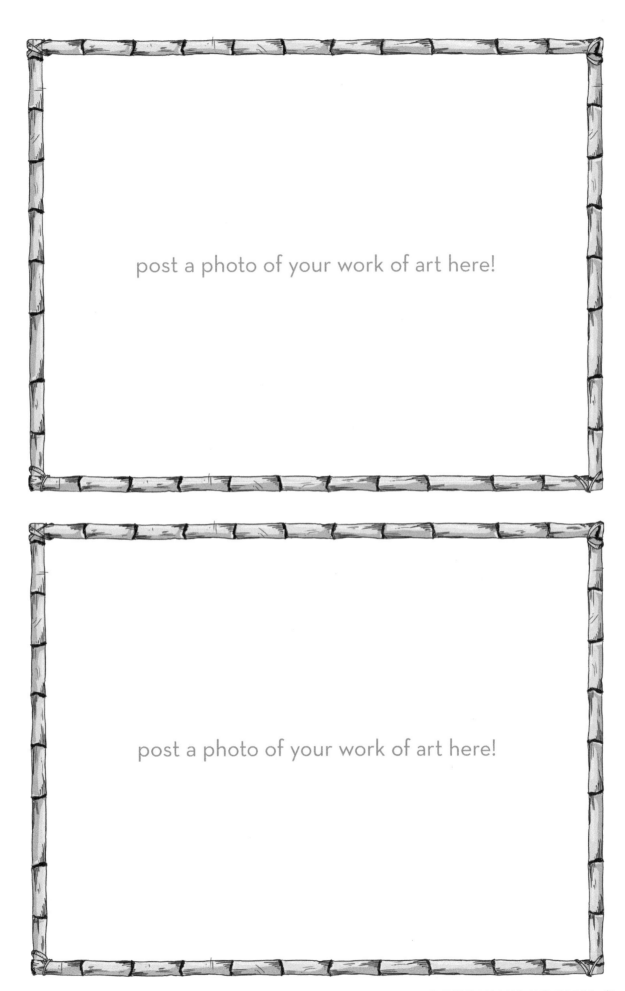

post a photo of your work of art here!

post a photo of your work of art here!

Journaling can be a way for all ages to process and integrate their experiences at home, school, work, and the community. For kids and teens, it's a great tool for exploring life experiences while learning mindfulness. Journaling works when it helps people make better sense of their experiences or find new meanings in it. Being able to think of one's experiences in a more organized, coherent, and constructive manner may reduce the associated emotional arousal and stress.

Age Range: 3–7 drawing journal; 8+ written journal

Materials

- Journal (homemade or store-bought)
- Writing materials (pens, markers, pencil crayons)

Directions

- **Choose a journal to suit you or your child's taste**. This can be a collection of paper, hole punched, with attractive string or ribbon holding it together. Or you can visit a local bookshop to hand-pick a journal.

- **Start your journaling practice by choosing a space and time** (garden, bed, school, coffee shop; morning, midmorning, afternoon, before bed). Begin with setting aside fifteen minutes a day for two days per week. This can be a solo activity or with a partner or a one-on-one activity with your adolescent for shared quiet time in each other's presence.

  - Journaling space: _____
  - Day 1: _____ at time: _____
  - Day 2: _____ at time: _____

- **Get writing, freestyle or prompted.** Try these journaling prompts if you don't know where to start:

  - Ways I was mindful today:
  - An act of kindness I witnessed today:
  - I'm grateful for …
  - An area I'd like to grow in:
  - What makes me unique:
  - How my best friend or partner would describe me:
  - What triggers [anger, joy, hunger, sadness, motivation, playfulness] in me:
  - One thing I like about myself and why:
  - If how I was feeling right now were a color, it would be _____; here's why:
  - Reflecting on the people in my life who have made me feel loved and supported, I feel grateful for …
  - This week, I intend to align my words, thoughts, and actions to these core values (visit page 140 for a list of core values):

- The top three feelings I wish to create, share, or experience with others around me today are _____, _____, and _____; here's why:

- **Make a decision to consciously journal.** Don't see journaling as another chore to get through or something you should do. Feel what you write and believe it. The fact that you can pause to reflect on your life experiences or make a list of things that make you feel grateful should make you feel, well, grateful.

- **Practice nonjudgment and flexibility while journaling.** Many set a minimum of five things to be grateful for or try to fill a page. Don't put yourself under pressure or take the joy out of journaling by being too regimented.

- **Make it a mindful doodling and drawing.** All ages can use a journal as an artistic outlet to explore their mindfulness journey. Try these doodle prompts if you don't know where to start:

  - Me being mindful:
  - Me *not* being mindful:
  - My family being mindful:
  - My family *not* being mindful:
  - My mind when *full* versus my mind when *mindful*:
  - Colors of my life:
  - Draw a bucket and draw pictures or doodle words of what brings you joy.

- **Get playful.** Who says journals are just a house for words? Include everything from concert tickets or wristbands to receipts from a memorable meal, photos of a family trip, or dried pressed flowers from a nature walk.

Science: Journaling, in the sense of writing about one's deepest thoughts and feelings, has been linked to both subjective and objective markers of health and well-being. Studies involving gratitude journals have determined that those who used one were more positive and happier. This style of journaling has been found to reduce annoyances, improve optimism, boost exercise patterns, and increase determination, attention, enthusiasm, and energy (Emmons and McCullough 2003).

I am grateful for

_____

Create: Peace Rocks

• • • • • • • • • • • • • • • • • • •

I've always been fascinated by rocks, collecting them on my father and grandmother's farm, shining them up, displaying them. I was fascinated by the million-year-old story the little pebbles had locked up within them. I carried a worry stone as a child that helped me when I was left on the playground to the very vivid moment I recall in the grade 4 public speech finals. In my practice, I've found children and parents alike gravitate to the steadiness and solidity of rocks. You can use rocks as a tool for mindfulness in your home. Whether you visit a local rock and gem shop or collect them on family walks, choose a bag as a family or per person as a dedicated mindful rock collection bag.

This exercise uses a rock for a mindful breathing and visualization. The tactile exploration of the rock together with a visualization of a mountain are used to explore the quality of solidity; the mountain knows it's solid no matter what's going on around it.

Age Range: 4+

Materials

- 1 rock per participant (you can have a bag of rocks if at home or select a rock from a hike in nature)

Directions

- **Choose your peace rock.** Each family member taking part chooses a pebble.

- **Tell the story of the rock.** Adult leading the activity will share the following (or personalized):

  - "This rock is the building block of the large vast mountains on earth, mountains that just sit there at all times, just being themselves, no matter the storms of snow, rain, or wind. We too can embody this unwavering stillness and rootedness in the face of chaos or changes in our lives."

- **Place the rock in your hand.** Demonstrate and continue to instruct:

  - "Now pick up the rock. Lay your hand flat like the surface of the earth on which mountains lie. Put your rock in the palm of your hand."

- **Explore the rock.** This is a free exploration where children and adults are encouraged to tap into their senses. Adults guiding the activity can also choose to use these exploration prompts and demonstrate:

  - "Investigate the rock with your eyes, noticing colors and how the rock reflects light."

- "Rub the rock between your hands for a few moments and then bring it to your nose to smell the mineral qualities."

- "Explore the textures, shapes, bumps, grooves, temperature, and weight of the rock with the touch of your fingers."

- **Hold the rock in stillness.** Everyone present wraps the hand holding the rock around it, the other palm supporting that hand. Close the eyes if comfortable. Sit in stillness, just breathing (for thirty seconds to three minutes). You can provide the following instructions:

  - "Now we are going to wrap our hands around the rock and close our eyes for a moment of stillness."

- **Visualize the mountain this rock once called home.** In this part of the exercise, we remain in stillness and visualize a mountain with our eyes closed, seeing it in all seasons, on sunny days and stormy days. You can provide the following guides for the visualization:

  - "Remaining in stillness with eyes closed, see the mountain this rock was a part of before it found its way into your palm. See the mountain in all seasons, resting in stillness, on sunny days and in blizzards. Notice the unwavering stillness of the mountain as you hear the wind howl or the cold snow on your skin, as well as the birds chirping and sun warming your skin."

- **Repeat a mantra for grounding.** With eyes open or closed, repeat the following mantra, aloud or silently, ten times:

  - [Inhale] "Breathing in, I see myself as a mountain."

  - [Pause, exhale] "Breathing out, I feel solid and peaceful."

Upgrade: Parents, pick up rocks yourself or encourage your child to collect rocks as part of a mindful walk or hike. Check out instructions on page X or X.

Create: Core Values

• • • • • • • • • • • • • • • • •

What's important to your family and to each person in it is unique and is worth exploring and celebrating. With this activity, your family will explore values, which are deeply held views of what we find worthwhile. Values come from many sources, including parents, religion, school, peers, and culture. Some we learn in childhood; others we learn as adults.

Age Range: 9+ and up

Materials

- Pen
- Paper
- Round wood slice (optional)
- Paint (optional)

Directions

- **Values 101.** Start by exploring the meaning of values, which are deeply held views of what one finds worthwhile. These can come from various sources: family, religion, school, culture.

- **Choose ten values.** From the values list, you and your participating family members choose ten words or phrases that are most important to yourselves. Encourage family members, and remind yourself, to think about the values listed and what they mean to you before picking them.

- **Narrow down to three values.** Next, really think about what's important to you by picking your top three out of the ten.

- **Complete the worksheet.** Once you have your three values, complete the worksheet.

- **Listen and discuss.** Listen and ask questions of your family members as they identify values. You can share stories about when you've seen your family member living their values.

- **Reflect**. Parents, after this activity, take a few moments together or solo to explore what you learned from this values conversation with your family.

- **Core values.** Get round wood slices (you can cut your own or purchase them at craft stores or online). Choose one or all three of your core values and paint the words on the wood slices. You can also choose to make this a family activity, where you choose a few core values that represent each family member and the family as a whole. You can use these handcrafted tools as coasters, nail them up on a wall, or display them in a shadow box or anywhere else you'll see them throughout the week.

exploring values

Teen + Adult Words

- accountability
- achievement
- balance (home/work)
- compassion
- competence
- communication
- cooperation
- courage
- creativity
- enthusiasm
- efficiency
- ethics
- excellence
- fairness
- family
- financial stability
- friendships
- fun
- health
- honesty
- independence
- integrity
- initiative
- making a difference
- personal fulfillment
- personal growth
- perseverance
- respect
- responsibility
- self-discipline
- spontaneity
- success
- trust

Kids Words/Phrases

- doing what you say you will
- reaching your goals
- balancing school/play time
- being kind and understanding
- being good at what you do
- talking openly with others
- working well with other people
- being brave
- using imagination
- being excited and confident
- making good use of time
- doing the right thing
- doing excellent in school/sport
- being fair
- family
- being smart with money
- having friends
- laughing and having fun
- keeping healthy
- telling the truth
- able to do things on your own
- being honest and trustworthy
- making decisions for yourself
- making life better for others
- having a full and happy life
- improving myself
- trying my best even when difficult
- showing respect
- being responsible
- controlling my behaviour
- trying something new
- being successful
- trusting others

Create: Mindful Jar

• • • • • • • • • • • • •

The mindful jar is often the first tool I use to introduce the concept of mindfulness to adults and kids alike. The mindful jar can be used by all ages as a mindful crafting practice, a visual teaching tool for what mindfulness is all about, as well as an object on which to meditate as one watches the glitter settle over time. In this exercise, you'll learn how to make the mindful jar, how to introduce it, when to use it, and where to store it:

Age Range: 3+ through adults

Materials

- A recycled plastic or glass water bottle or jar with labels removed
- 1 small bottle clear, nontoxic glue to fill ⅓ of jar
- Warm water to fill ⅔ of jar
- 1 Tbsp+ glitter in various colors (look for a sample or mixed pack)
- Small plastic toy or small meaningful memento
- 1–2 drops food coloring (optional)

Directions for Making the Mindful Jar

- **Start with filling the jar with glue.** Choose your bottle and fill it approximately ⅓ full with clear glue. Note: the more glue you add, the longer the glitter will move around the jar before settling at the bottom.

- **Add water.** You want to add approximately ⅔ the volume of your jar with warm or hot water. Mind the temperature of the water when making with young children.

- **Add glitter.** Measure roughly 1 Tbsp or more of glitter and add to the jar.

- **Add optional punch of color.** This is not a necessary step, given the glitter will add lots of color to the mindful jar, but some like to have a pop of color in their jar. Add 1–2 drops of food coloring.

- **Shake**. Gently shake the jar or store with a spoon to combine the glue, water, and glitter.

- **Fill 'er up.** Add water to fill the remaining space in the jar.

- **Seal the mindful jar.** Use a hot glue gun to close the lid or cap of the mindful jar.

Directions for Using the Mindful Jar with Kids

- **Introduce the mindful jar.** The first time you introduce the mindful jar, hold the jar in front of the child. Ask:

- "Can you see the toy inside the jar?"

- **Shake the jar.** After shaking the jar, engage with the following:

  - "Can you see the toy inside the jar?" [Likely answer will be no, to which you can provide an explanation similar to the following:] "This is what happens when we are worried and angry, and our feelings and thoughts are whirling around."

- **Practice patiently watching.** Next, encourage them to do nothing but simply watch the jar as the contents of the jar starts to settle. Provide an explanation similar to the following:

  - "This is what mindful breathing does for the mind—it clears the mind and settles our big feelings and thoughts, helping us feel better."

- **Get moving.** Next instruct your child to wiggle their body or jump up and down or twirl around. Meanwhile, shake the mindful jar or let them hold it. Say:

  - "Is your mind and body revved up again? See how the water is cloudy again, just like your mind when you're busy? Let's sit and watch and breathe. When you see the water clear up again and you can clearly see the toy, silently raise your hand."

- **Teach how breath can help settle body-heart-mind.** Say to the children:

  - "Breathing slowly and steadily can help your big thoughts and feelings settle, and your mind and body will become more calm."

- **Keep up the mindful jar practice.** After the first demonstration, have this as a tool your child can use to practice mindful awareness and to help calm down when overwhelmed, angry, or afraid. Encourage them to hold it, shake it, and then find stillness as they watch the glitter settle.

Directions for Use of the Mindful Jar with Teens and Adults

- **Same, same.** For adults and teens, the instructions are much the same. The swirling glitter is very calming as it falls to the bottom of the bottle, for both kids and adults. Teens and adults may not feel the desire to jump up and down and twirl, but they can just shake the bottle and practice sitting and having the sight of the bottle and breath be the focal point of mindful awareness.

- **In heated family moments.** If your family finds itself in a heated moment, the mindful jar can be used to encourage mindful communication. Parents, try saying the following, with aid of the mindful jar:

  - "We're all upset. We all have lots of thoughts and big feelings right now. Let's take a break until the glitter in the mindful jar has settled. Then let's start talking again."

Explore: You can also use a snow globe to illustrate this concept and do this practice.

Create: Tech Bed

● ● ● ● ● ● ● ● ● ● ● ● ● ● ●

Do you or your children struggle to put your phone to sleep at night so you can do the same? Research has proven smart phones are addictive and can disrupt your sleep. Try out this family DIY activity for making a phone basket or bed for all ages, whether just for the family or for a get-together with family or friends. Make one big bed for co-sleeping family phones, or have an individual bed for each family member's phone.

Let your phones recharge so you can recharge.

Age Range: Children, teens, and adults who have tablets or cell phones

Materials

- A box (wine crate, small craft box, or office organizing box)
- Chalk label or permanent marker that will write on the chosen container.
- A counter away from rooms where the tech bed can find a permanent home.

Directions

- Choose a container that will fit all your family's technology devices that need a rest at night. Our family uses the soft fabric closet drawer organizers, as those are large and won't scratch devices.

- Set a bedtime for technology at night. You may use the bedtime you've set out in the tech contract on page 47-49. At tech bedtime, power down your tech and plug in if necessary.

- For younger children, they can sing a lullaby.

- Tech shouldn't leave the tech bed until the family's agreed-upon wake/use time.

Create: Homemade Gifts

· · · · · · · · · · · · · · ·

Sometimes I go with the gift card, once taboo but now a go-to for gifting. But there's something about a homemade gift. It is a chance to get creative and put a personal touch on a gift for someone. And for the receiver, there is often a moment of pause, reflecting on how someone carved out time from modern lives that get very full just for them. In a word, homemade gifts are mindful for giver and receiver. These are two of our family's favorite small gifts to give:

Trail Mix

Visit page 200-201 and choose one of the fun themed trail mixes. The ingredients and materials needed are likely found in your kitchen or office. Get playful and feel good knowing you're giving the gift of nourishment.

Materials

- Clear glass jar with lid.
- Custom trail mix blend (see page 200-201 for trail mix ideas).
- Ribbon, twine, or string, to add a decorative touch around the neck of the jar and to attach a tag to.
- A gift tag. You can use one you have in the house or cut out the shape of gift tag from cardstock. On one side, print TO and FROM. On the other side, include all the ingredients in the jar.
- You may also consider writing a positive affirmation about the receiver on a tiny piece of paper and hide inside the trail mix for them to discover later.

Relax Kit

Do you have a mama or papa friend who could use a little relaxation in their life? (I don't know anyone who'd say no). Below are all the materials that likely you can find around your house from the kitchen to the office to the bathroom. Once all materials are gathered, thoughtfully arrange the basket or bag.

Materials

- Basket or gift bag.
- A couple individually wrapped herbal tea bags.
- A mason jar filled with Epsom salts.
- A vial of essential oils (see page 115 for essential oil blends).
- A handwritten note that can have a quote or personal thought to induce calm and relaxation in the receiver. This could even be a suggestion for a meditation app that you feel the receiver may be interested in using.
- Nice paper for printing instructions for essential oil bath salt crafting (see page 115).

Eat and Drink

· · · · · · · · · · · · · · ·

Eat and Drink: Introduction

• • • • • • • • • • • • • •

It's not just what you eat, but also how you eat that affects your mental and physical health. Many parents and kids are on the go between childcare drop-off, gym, work, meet-ups with friends, play dates, soccer practice, grocery shopping, meal prep, the bank, and so on. So rushed, mindless eating happens. And that's okay; I'm in the same boat numerous times a week. It's not about being perfect, remember.

Many families today are using mindfulness as a tool to help discover a richer relationship with life that includes a healthy relationship with one's family and food. Mindful eating simply means being present during the act of eating instead of being distracted by TV or having the mind wander. It involves using all of the senses to truly take in the eating experience. In mindful eating, we're not comparing or judging. We're simply witnessing the many sensations, thoughts, and emotions that come up around preparing food, eating food, cleaning up after a meal or snack, and digesting.

Mindful, or intuitive, eating practices offer up benefits you and your kids can really sink your teeth into, daily. Mindful eating is a tool used by parents to curb picky eating. It also helps reduce overeating and binge eating, reduce anxious thoughts about food and your body, regulate eating habits, and manage weight effectively.

Did I mention that mindful eating doesn't just benefit mind and body but can also be fun? Flip through this section to learn nutritional and mindful eating tips for fast, colorful, nourishing beverages and food for the whole family. The recipes have been carefully curated based on what I've found my family likes but also what's a hit at experiential family food events I host and among families I see in therapy. They range from how parents can make and mindfully sip a butter coffee to chocolate meditations for the whole family, and of course fun ways to get picky little eaters (and parents) to stop shedding tears at the dinner table.

Ready to pause and play with your food?

• • • • • • • • • • • •

Eat and Drink: Mindful Eating Intention Setting

What would you like to build, create, or nurture in your relationship with your food and body?

_____

_____

What would you like to let go of in your relationship with your food and body?

_____

_____

What would you like your children or partner to let go of in their relationship with food and the body?

_____

_____

When are you _most_ mindful while eating (note places, times, people around you, type of food)?

_____

_____

When are you _least_ mindful while eating (note places, times, people around you, type of food)?

_____

_____

What food would you most like to play with?

_____

_____

Eat and Drink: Let's Talk Hunger and Fullness

• • • • • • • • • • • • • •

The concepts of hunger and fullness seem simple enough. You likely hear your child saying one extreme or the other frequently throughout the day. Hunger is a natural way for your body to remind you to eat; it's as simple as that.

Mindful eating involves continually determining how hungry or full you are before, during, and after you've eaten. The hunger and fullness scale helps you evaluate your relative hunger and fullness, giving you an inner navigational guide to eating. The scale runs from 0 to 10, 0 being the hunger level at which you feel empty and sick, 10 being the fullness level at which you feel painfully full or ill. The goal is to not go below 3 or beyond a 7 on the scale. This is a zone of slight hunger or fullness, where one is comfortable.

I encourage you to listen to your own body to figure out where you are on this scale and ask your children what is happening in their body telling them they are hungry or full. And don't forget, being mindful means being free of judgment. We all overeat sometimes because food just tastes good and we're enjoying ourselves, which is okay. Let it go.

hunger + fullness scale

0	1	2	3	4	5	6	7	8	9	10
empty, feel sick	ravenous, irritable	very hungry	hunger pangs	slightly hungry	neutral	slightly full	satisfied	very full	uncomfort-ably full	full, feeling sick

Directions for Use of the Hunger and Fullness Scale with Teens and Adults

- **Check in before a meal.** Evaluate how hungry you are before you begin eating.

- **Check in during your meal.** When you've eaten half your snack or meal, pause, put down your utensils, and check in with your hunger and fullness. Are you approaching 7 on the fullness scale? How do you think you will feel if you eat past this point? If you decide to continue to eat, eat as slowly and mindfully as possible.

- **Check in after your meal.** Notice where you are on the scale. Are you comfortably full at a 7? Are you painfully full at a 9 or 10? If you're contemplating getting up for more food, wait five minutes and assess your hunger level again.

Directions for Use of the Hunger and Fullness Scale with Kids

- **Check in before a meal.** Ask your children if they are hungry or full. Ask them where in their body from head to toe is telling them they are hungry or full.

- **Check in at the "I'm full" point.** When your children say they are full, ask where in their body is telling them they are full. Ask what it feels like to be full. Thank them for listening to their body.

Eat and Drink: Mindful Breathing and Eating Meditation Practice

• • • • • • • • • • • • •

Here is a mindful breathing and eating practice your family can do at home a couple times per week:

Mindful Prep for Eating (Two Minutes)

Use the following script to guide yourself and your children through this exercise to prepare for a mindful eating practice.

- Let your body rest comfortably in a chair. Notice your legs and feet. Relax them.

- Close your eyes.

- Notice your shoulders, arms, and hands. Let the tension out of them. Relax your hands and arms; let your shoulders sink into a relaxed state.

- Do diaphragmatic breathing (review belly breathing **basics on** page 53).

- Place a hand on your belly so you can feel the air come in and go out.

- Now focus on your breath. Slowly breathe air into your body through your nose or mouth. Like a wave, fill your chest and then belly, feeling each rise as it fills with air.

- When your belly is full, slowly exhale; empty air from your belly, feeling it get smaller.

- Continue to slowly move the air out through your mouth.

- Repeat the breathing process. Then open eyes and begin the mindful eating activity.

Inhale Air not Food

Mindful Eating Practice (Four Minutes)

Select a food, such as a raisin, orange segment, apple slice, chocolate squeal, or other small piece of food on a plate. Place the plate in front of yourself and your child. Take your child through the script below, varying it as you feel appropriate.

- Look at the [food's name].

- What is its shape?

- What size is it?

- What color is it?

- What smell do you notice?

- What sensation do you notice in your mouth as you look at it?

- What's the feeling in your stomach?

- Now pick up the food slowly. Hold it in your fingers and look at it in your grasp. What does it feel like in your hand: its texture, temperature?

- Bring it slowly to your lips.

- Before putting the food into your mouth, pause and be aware of what you're experiencing in your mouth. Slowly open and place the food on your tongue for a moment without biting into it. Feel what you mouth wants to do with it.

- Take a few moments before you bite into it. Feel its texture on your tongue and in your mouth. What do you taste?

- Now bite into it, noticing what you taste and what it feels like. As you continue to taste, try not to swallow the food right away. Does the taste and feeling change as you're chewing? Feel the food going down as you swallow. Refocus on your mouth. Notice your stomach and what it's feeling. You've now finished the exercise; well done.

Eat and Drink: Top Mindful Eating Tips

• • • • • • • • • • • •

Mindful eating requires you to be in the moment and to deliberately pay attention. Not only to the act of eating, but also preparing the food, waiting for it to cook, setting the table, and washing the dishes. For children and teens who start to eat mindfully, it could mean they may eat less often (when hungry rather than out of habit or from emotions), and they may eat less and hopefully desire healthier foods. Here are tips for integrating mindful eating practices into your daily routine:

Rate Your Hunger

Rate your hunger. Before, during, and after a meal, tap into your hunger and fullness levels. Rate on a scale of 1 to 10 as described on pages 148-149.

Identify Your Hunger

Is it a physical need or emotional desire? If emotional, notice the feelings that are coming up within you and what foods you're craving. If eating out, notice if you bank calories or skip meals leading up to dining out; this is maladaptive and can lead to overeating.

Declutter

As you go to prepare a meal, take away distractions and clutter from the kitchen. Your kids can help with age-appropriate kitchen tidying. This may mean washing the dirty dishes or clearing food prep surfaces. A clean kitchen will help you prepare your family's meal mindfully.

Sit Down Free of Distractions

Whether having a snack or a meal, always sit when eating in the kitchen or dining room or even outdoors on a chair or blanket. Reduce distractions such as television or cell phones or music. This helps focus on the eating experience and supports you checking in to assess hunger and fullness levels more accurately.

Tap into Your Senses

Mindful eating is an experience that engages the five senses. By using your senses, you'll appreciate all the characteristics of the food. You and your children are more likely to savor the bites, eat slower, digest better, and enjoy the meal more. Look at your food; notice the colors. Notice the different scents your food offers. Feel the bursts of flavors as you place food in your mouth, be it sour, salty, bitter, sweet, rich, spicy. Listen to the sound of your jaw and the food as you chew your food, whether it's crunchy, chewy, tough, sticky. Notice the weight of the food on your tongue. Draw awareness to the texture and shape; is it hard or soft? Creamy or smooth? Does it have ridges? Is it rounded?

So when eating, remember and remind family members to look, smell, taste, touch, and listen.

Slow the Fork Down

When using utensils, take your bite in your mouth. Then put your eating utensils down and place your hands on your lap between bites. If you find it difficult to slow down and bring awareness to your hands on your utensils, try switching up your utensils to your nondominant hand.

Be Chewsy

Chew your bite of food with laser-sharp focus. Practice chewing until your food becomes uniformly liquid (for adults, try taking thirty or more bites). When we chew, our bodies secrete enzymes that help break down food and signal digestion to begin.

Set the Mood

When you're about to do food prep or sit down for a meal, turn the TV off, put on music that relaxes you and assists in getting you to a more mindful place (for some, this may mean classical music; others may prefer acoustic rock).

Breathe

Before you eat, take three deep breaths; in through your nose, out through your mouth. This allows you to relax and feel more grounded. It also shifts your parasympathetic nervous system into a resting state, so your body can digest your meal and receive maximum nutrition from it.

Give Gratitude

Give gratitude for all those who've had a hand in your meal. If eating with your family, do this aloud, reflecting on the farmers, truck drivers, market vendors, and all others between farm and table who've made your meal possible. Check out page 154 for a mindful eating chant that involves practicing gratitude. Then be mindful of your body, expressing gratitude for its ability to receive a nourishing meal.

Don't Pass on the Passeggiata

After your meal, take a passeggiata (leisurely walk, in Italian) to help you digest and transition from your eating experience. It can be a perfect ending to an enjoyable meal on your own or with friends and family. Check out the mindful walk instructions on pages 90-91.

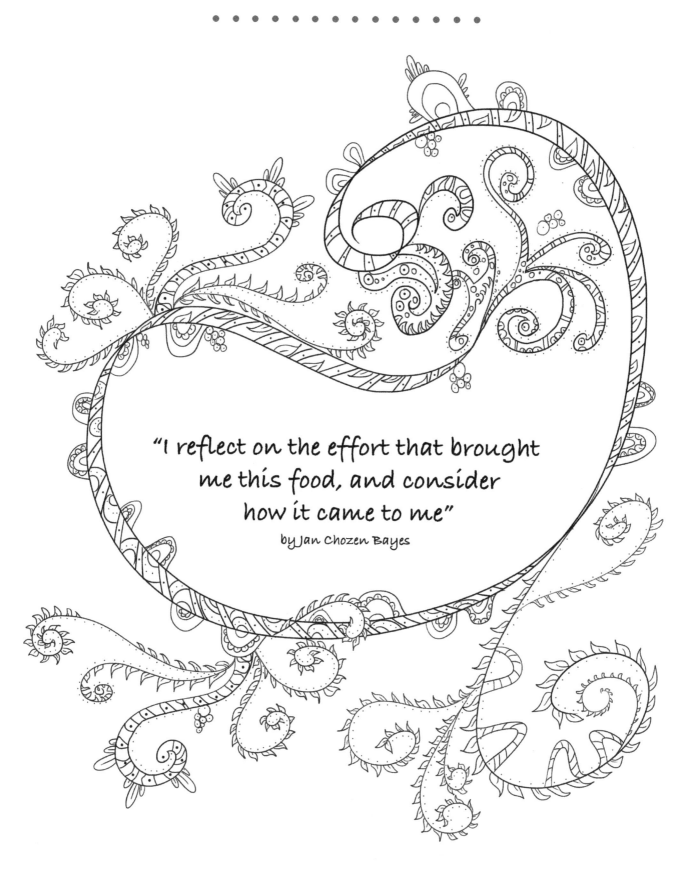

"I reflect on the effort that brought me this food, and consider how it came to me"

by Jan Chozen Bayes

Eat and Drink: Mindful Family Feast

• • • • • • • • • • • • • •

We know reducing distractions when eating and curating a relationship with food around joy, gratitude, and curiosity is beneficial for all ages. You no doubt have heard the many benefits of a shared family meal. But I propose taking it a step further; mindful eating is an opportunity for both connecting and bringing a healthy dose of mindfulness to everyone in the family at the same time, doing the routine activity of eating dinner.

Studies link regular family meals with behaviors most parents want for their children: improved academic performance, higher grade-point averages, better resilience, and more self-esteem. Additionally, family meals are linked to lower rates of substance abuse, teen pregnancy, eating disorders, and depression.

Mindful Eating Conversation Starters

Teaching your children to focus on the food at the family table, while also doing it yourself, can be beneficial for the whole family (brains and bodies). You can focus the conversation around the food or enjoy fun, mindful eating games with your kids.

Explore these questions and prompts:

- Discuss where you are on the hunger scale before, midway through, and after a meal.

- Describe the smell of your food before you taste it.

- Try to name the spice or seasoning in the dish.

- Name the vegetables you see on the plate.

- What's your favorite part of this meal?

- What's your least favorite part of this meal?

- Can you describe the texture of your first bite?

- How far has this food traveled to reach this table?

- How many people do you think were involved in bringing this food to our table?

- What are the benefits of organic foods?

- Is it ethical to eat animals?

Explore: Check out the Family Dinner Project website (www.familydinnerproject.org). It's a nonprofit organization operating out of Harvard University.

Eat and Drink: Picky Eater to Mindful Eater

• • • • • • • • • • • • • •

Are your little ones challenging at mealtime, making the concept of a mindful meal laughable or a distant prospect?

Defining Picky Eating

Based on research, I view kids in two picky eating categories: passing and persistent. Here's a simple way to tell whether your child's picky eating is passing or persistent. The majority of children who consume thirty or more foods are usually considered to be in the more common "passing pickiness" category. Passing pickiness includes food jags, refusals, and other difficulties that may change over time. Some children's eating habits change in response to family dynamics (separation, moving, arrival of a newborn). Children who eat twenty foods or fewer are referred to as "persistent picky" eaters. Persistent pickiness tends to be based on physical characteristics (oral motor sensitivities caused by premature birth, autism spectrum disorders, and genetic predispositions to some flavors).

Note: if your child is a persistent picky eater, consult with your doctor or ask your pediatrician for an appropriate referral.

Mindful Eating Tips for Picky Eaters

Here are a number of practices you can bring into the home to support your child in exploring foods mindfully:

- **Division of labor.** A basic mindful eating guide involves parents providing the food and children deciding how much of the offerings they want to eat. If your children have a clean bill of health from the family doctor or pediatrician, you can rest assured they are not going to starve by expressing pickiness during a meal and eating little.

- **Pause**. As the mantra earlier in this book suggests, pause, then parent. It's helpful for you to pause when your children challenge your patience. Simply take a few deep breaths before reacting. Nearly seventy years of research supports pausing under a variety of technical terms.

- **Children as carbon copies.** Parents who enjoy their meals, keep to meal schedules, and do not bring tech to the table are mindful eating role models.

- **Keep the peace at the table.** Do the best you can to allow your family to eat in serenity. Parents who are calm and caring help children feel safe. Pushing food on children can activate hormones that suppress their appetite.

- **Mind the appetite disrupters.** Your child's appetite can be affected by too much juice, anticipating an event, worries, or a cold.

- **Keep trying.** The research varies, but know that it can take upwards of fifteen times for children to be exposed to, try, and decide if they like particular new foods. Patience is a mindful mama or papa's virtue when it comes to parenting picky eaters.

Eat and Drink: Mind Your Microbiome

• • • • • • • • • • • • • • • • •

Mindful eating in my personal practice includes attending to my moods and how those can be impacted by the foods I eat. And also being conscious of the mood and food intersection for the rest of the family, including the kids. Enter the microbiome.

What Is the Microbiome?

Our microbiome consists of trillions of microorganisms (also called microbiota) of thousands of species (Ursell et al. 2012). These include bacteria, fungi, parasites, and viruses. In a healthy individual, the "bugs" peacefully coexist, mostly in the small and large intestines. The microbiome promotes the smooth daily operations of the human body.

You're first exposed to microorganisms as an infant, during delivery in the birth canal and through your mother's breast milk. Environmental exposures and diet can change your microbiome to be beneficial to your health or put you at greater risk for disease.

How Microbiota Benefit the Body

Our microbiota stimulate the immune system, break down potentially toxic compounds, and synthesize vitamins and amino acids. Complex carbohydrates like starches and fibers are not as easily digested and may travel lower to the large intestine. There, microbiota help break down these compounds with their digestive enzymes. The microbiota of a healthy person also provides protection from pathogenic organisms that enter the body through drinking contaminated water or eating bad food.

Can Diet Affect One's Microbiota?

In addition to family genes, environment, and medication use, diet plays a big role in determining what kinds of microbiota live in your body. Foods that support healthy probiotic growth are indigestible carbohydrates and fibers such as resistant starches. These fibers are sometimes called prebiotics because they feed our beneficial microbiota.

Eat and Drink: Mandala Colouring Page

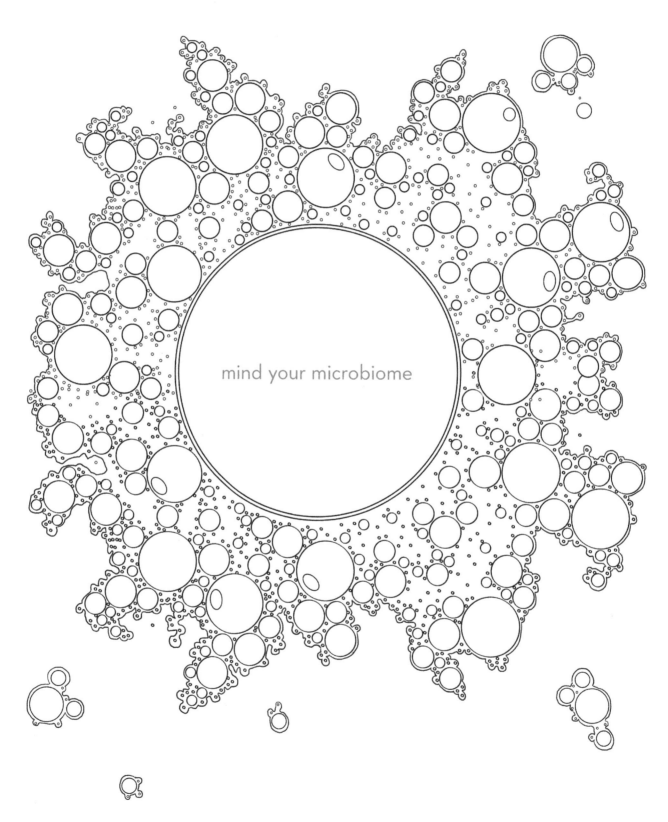

mind your microbiome

Probiotic Foods

Probiotic powders and fermented supplements now abound in the health food market. But if you don't have a medical condition requiring probiotic supplementation or medication, getting probiotics from the food in your diet is optimal. Probiotic foods contain beneficial live microbiota that can further enhance your microbiome. These include fermented foods like kefir (water- or yogurt-based), yogurt with live active cultures, pickled vegetables (unpasteurized and pickled in brine), tempeh, fermented meat/fish/eggs, kombucha tea, kimchi, miso, kraut (any variety, from cabbage to beet to carrot), and cultured condiments (lacto-fermented mayonnaise, mustard, horseradish, hot sauce, relish, salsa, guacamole, salad dressing).

Prebiotic Foods

Although there are supplements containing prebiotic fibers, there are many healthful foods naturally containing prebiotics. The highest amounts are found in raw versions of the following: garlic, onions, leeks, asparagus, Jerusalem artichokes, dandelion greens, bananas, and seaweed. In general, fruits, vegetables, beans, and whole grains like wheat, oats, and barley are all good sources of prebiotic fibers. Be aware that high intake of prebiotic foods, especially if introduced suddenly, can increase gas production and bloating.

Eat and Drink: WaterFull

It's time to bring mindfulness to something as simple as a glass of water. Whipping up a batch of infused water at home is simple (and mouth-watering).

Science: Water is essential for life. Without water, humans cannot survive for more than a few days. Water helps your body keep its temperature normal, protects your spinal cord and other sensitive tissues, lubricates and cushions joints, and gets rid of wastes through urination, perspiration, and bowel movements (Popkin, D'Anci, and Rosenberg 2011).

Infused Water Inspiration

It's easy to prep thirst-quenching flavorful water infusions; all you'll need is water and fresh fruit, vegetables, or herbs. For the fresh herbs, a tip I learned at Spotted Bear Distillery, a craft distillery in Montana, is to put your fresh herbs in one hand and slap your hands together a few times to release the plant essence.

Try one of these recipes or create your own twist on a glass of water. Note: these recipes are great right away but have more developed taste after a few hours to a day in the fridge.

- **Citrus Zing:** juice of ½ orange and slices from remaining ½ orange

- **Refresher**: handful of fresh mint leaves and ½ cup sliced cucumber

- **Berry Blast**: muddled and whole berries (your choice: blueberries, strawberries, huckleberries, raspberries, blackberries)

- **Ch-Ch-Ch-Chia and Cherry**: 1 Tbsp chia seeds and ⅔ cup cherry halves

- **Tropical Twist:** ¼ pineapple peeled and thinly sliced and handful of smashed mint leaves and squirt of lime juice

- **Summer Water:** 2 cups finely chopped watermelon and handful of smashed basil and water

- **Grape Ade:** 2 cups halved grapes and 1 thinly sliced orange

Eat and Drink: Nut Mylk

• • • • • • • • • • • • • • • •

The idea of making homemade nut mylk at first sounded to me just as daunting as strapping on some overalls, pulling on rubber boots, and trekking out to a neighboring pasture behind my house in Springbank to milk a cow.

That all changed when I went to a demo class at the Light Cellar, a local superfood and elixir bar. Life changing may be an overstatement, but seeing how easy it was and how calming watching the mylk strain down into the mason jar was pretty profound. It hit me that this would be a great meditation for myself but also a good activity to teach kitchen skills and use as a calming tool for my young children.

I'm not anti store-bought nut mylk (you'll still find it in my house from time to time). But parents who make their own nut mylk at home have plenty to look forward to. For starters, you'll be saving on your grocery bill, especially if you buy nuts in bulk. Nut mylk recipes are also easy and can be adjusted, and kids can take it on as a tasty weekly chore. It can be a creative endeavour, where you try various flavors, from maple walnut to macacino to salted caramel cashew milk.

Ingredients

- 1 cup nuts (almonds, hazelnuts, pistachios, pecans, walnuts, cashews, or peanuts)
- 4 cups of water and water for soaking nuts
- 4 tsp sweetener of choice (optional; honey, maple syrup, coconut sugar, agave nectar)
- ¼ tsp salt

Directions

- **Choose your nuts**. Place nuts in a large bowl. Add water to cover by 2 inches.
- **Soak and drain.** Let stand at least 12 hours. The longer the nuts soak, the smoother the milk will be. Drain nuts and discard soaking liquid.
- **Blend**. Purée nuts, sweetener, salt, and 4 cups hot water (not boiling) in a blender on high speed until very smooth (approximately 2 minutes).
- **Strain**. Place a fine-mesh sieve or nut mylk bag into a medium bowl or large mason jar. Strain the nut milk by pressing the solids down slowly.
- **Set nut pulp aside.** Some people throw it away, but I don't like wasting food. You can use in cookies, bars, crackers, and other baked goods. You can also use it as compost in the garden.
- **Thin**. Add enough water to the nut mylk to reach desired consistency.
- **Store**. Transfer to airtight container and keep chilled.

Explore: Check out the dehydrated ginger snap cookie recipe on page 206. This recipe is a great way to use the pulp left over from your homemade nut mylk preparation.

Eat and Drink: Better Butter Coffee

• • • • • • • • • • • • • •

Taken from the Tibetan tradition of butter tea, butter coffee is taking the wellness world by storm. For a beverage that most parents rely on after late nights and early mornings with kids, work, and all the other activities of a full life, coffee is often held with clutched hands in high esteem. Here you'll learn the nutrition of coffee, tips of mindfully drinking coffee, and recipes for various versions of the Better Butter Coffee.

Age Range: Adults

Ingredients

- 1–2 Tbsp unsalted grass-fed butter
- 1–2 Tbsp XCT Oil
- 1–2 cups (250–500 milliliters) of hot coffee brewed with organic or low toxin beans

Directions

- **Brew**. Prepare your coffee as you normally would.

- **Preheat blender.** Boil extra water and pour it into a blender while your coffee brews to preheat the blender.

- **Froth**. Dump out the hot water from the now preheated blender and add the brewed coffee, butter, and XCT oil. Blend until there is a thick layer of foam on top like a latte. The stronger the blender, the better (a spoon won't work).

- **Upgrade.** Try one of the optional recipes below.

  - Base: 1 Tbsp grass-fed butter and 1 Tbsp coconut oil and 1 cup organic coffee
  - Vegan Base: 1 Tbsp organic almond butter and 1 Tbsp coconut oil and 1 cup organic coffee
  - Pro Upgrade: 2 Tbsp collagen or vegan protein powder
  - Spa Upgrade: fresh lavender or edible lavender essential oil
  - Pepped-Up Coffee: fresh peppermint leaves or peppermint essential oil
  - Spicy Sip: 1 tsp cinnamon and 1 tsp turmeric
  - Haute Chocolate: small dash of chili pepper and ½ Tbsp cocoa powder

Always consult with a health care professional before ingesting essential oils.

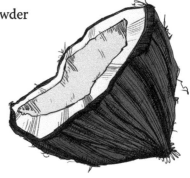

Eat and Drink: Maca Mocha

• • • • • • • • • • • • •

Maca root is an ancient ingredient that in modern days is most often used in powdered form in smoothies, cooking, baking, and roasting. It has a scent similar to butterscotch. Below is a recipe for 1 serving of a maca mocha you can have in the morning or midday.

Age Range: Adults

Ingredients

- 1 cup nut mylk (or other milk preference)
- ½ Tbsp maple syrup or 1 package of stevia or other sweetener
- 1 Tbsp maca powder
- 1 Tbsp cocoa powder
- 1 Tbsp coconut oil
- 1 tsp cinnamon
- Pinch of salt
- 1 cup coffee (optional, add more frothed nut mylk if not adding coffee)

Directions

- **Heat**. Warm your nut mylk as desired (milk frother, microwave, stovetop).

- **Blend**. Put nut mylk and all other ingredients in a blender suitable for hot beverages. Blend until frothed.

Note: This mocha has a good energizing kick to it without the coffee, hence it being an optional ingredient.

History: Maca root is a plant native to Peru that's been used as a medicinal herb in the Andes Mountains for more than two thousand years.

Science: Maca root contains potassium, calcium, magnesium, copper, zinc, and phytosterols. Some of the reported medicinal uses include enhancing energy, mental focus, stamina, athletic performance, memory, arousal, and fertility; treating female hormone imbalance, menstrual problems, and symptoms of menopause; and boosting the immune system (Health Canada 2012; Sandoval et al. 2002).

Explore: Try addicting maca to other recipes for a nutty, malted flavor.

Eat and Drink: Savory Bone Broth Latte

• • • • • • • • • • • • • •

All bone broths—beef, chicken, fish, lamb, and more—are staples in the traditional diets of every culture. That's because bone broths are nutrient-dense, easy to digest, and rich in flavor, and they boost healing of the gut/reduce inflammation. The aroma of this latte and the first burst of flavor will comfort an ill child or adult, provide a nourishing break midday or after a day on the ski hill. The following recipe makes 2 servings.

Ingredients

- 3 cups free-range chicken or turkey bone broth
- 2 Tbsp grass-fed butter or ghee
- 2 Tbsp coconut oil
- Garnish with small handful of fresh or a pinch of dried savory herbs (sage, thyme, rosemary)

Directions

- **Heat**. Warm the bone broth on your stovetop.

- **Blend**. Add all ingredients to a blender that is safe for hot beverages. Blend on high for 20–45 seconds.

History: Bone broth, or stock, was a way our ancestors made use of every part of an animal.

Science: Bones and marrow, skin and feet, tendons and ligaments that you can't eat directly can be boiled and then simmered over a period of days. This simmering causes the bones and ligaments to release healing compounds like collagen, proline, glycine, and glutamine. Further, bone broths contain minerals in forms that your body can easily absorb: calcium, magnesium, phosphorus, silicon, sulfur, and others. Of particular interest to me as a psychologist is the gelatin found in bone broth. It's beneficial for restoring strength of the gut lining, helps with growth of probiotics (good bacteria) in the gut, and supports healthy inflammation levels in the digestive tract. As we know, the gut is our second brain, and healthy guts make for healthy brains.

Eat and Drink: Night-Turm Latte

• • • • • • • • • • • • • • •

For an easy-to-prepare turmeric latte, you can use premade blends for turmeric lattes found at many health food stores. Or you can make it from scratch in your own kitchen. The following recipe makes 1 serving. While you can have this latte any time of the day, I personally love it as a soothing treat after putting the toddlers to bed, which helps me transition to my own bedtime.

Ingredients

- ¾ tsp organic turmeric, ground
- ½ tsp organic ginger, ground
- ½ tsp organic cinnamon, ground
- ½ tsp organic nutmeg, ground
- ½ tsp ashwagandha
- 1 tsp organic blackstrap molasses
- 1 Tbsp coconut oil
- Pinch of salt and black pepper
- 1½ cups of coconut milk (or other milk preference)
- Serve topped with pinch of nutmeg

Directions

- **Heat**. Warm the preferred liquid on the stovetop or in the microwave.

- Add all ingredients to a blender that's safe for hot beverages. If using golden mylk mix, just add the molasses and nutmeg listed above.

- Blend on high for 20–45 seconds, until smooth and frothy.

Science: Ashwagandha is reported to boost immunity, improve memory, decrease stress and anxiety levels in adults, and may improve quality of life. In one research study, supplementation was shown to increase muscle mass and strength alongside a resistance training program. Nutmeg is also an ingredient worth highlighting. Traditional healing practitioners and modern health providers and researchers are now using it for its mild sedative action and in treating insomnia.

Eat and Drink: Smoothies

• • • • • • • • • • • • • • • •

These smoothies are portioned for two adults and two kids, unless otherwise noted. The flavors are kid taste-tested and approved, meeting all the needs of mood- and food-supporting snacks and meals.

The Three-Ingredient Smoothie

Doesn't get much easier than three ingredients in a smoothie. This one is kid and adult taste-tested and approved. To better suit to particular taste buds, explore the optional add-ins.

Ingredients

- ¼ avocado
- ½ banana (fresh or frozen)
- ½ cup milk or milk alternative
- Optional add-ins:
    - ¼ cup frozen or fresh berries
    - ½ small peach or apple
    - ¼ mango
    - Handful of frozen or fresh baby spinach or kale
    - 1 tbsp nut or seed butter
    - 1 tsp maple syrup or honey
    - Dash of cinnamon
    - 2 tsp molasses
    - ¼ cup oats

Directions

- Blend all ingredients until smooth.

Brainy Smoothie

This is a smoothie recipe full of ingredients for brain health.

Ingredients

- 1 cup coconut milk
- 2–3 cups water (based on preference)
- 3 cups frozen organic blueberries
- 1 avocado
- 2 organic bananas
- 2 Tbsp honey

- Vanilla protein powder (optional, for adults)
- Ice (optional)

Directions

- Blend all ingredients until smooth.
- If not being consumed right away, put all ingredients other than the coconut milk and water and ice in freezer bag; pull out and put in fridge night before consuming/blending.

Science: Did you know blueberries pack a whole slew of brain-benefiting qualities? Research with human and animal subjects has shown blueberry consumption may prevent age-related memory loss, as well as boost concentration, memory, and even brain cell count.

Choco-Cado Smoothie

The richness of chocolate and the smooth velvety texture of the avocado has this smoothie on par with the experience of a decadent dessert!

Ingredients

- 3 organic bananas
- 1½ avocado
- 6 Tbsp cocoa powder
- 1 cup oats
- 1 cup plain Greek yogurt (fermented coconut yogurt or soy yogurt works as dairy-free substitute)
- 3 cups milk or milk alternative
- Ice (optional)

Directions

- Blend all ingredients until smooth.
- If not being consumed right away, put all ingredients other than the milk and yogurt and ice in a freezer bag; pull out and put in fridge night before consuming/blending.

Sunshine Smoothie

This smoothie was the product of a morning playing in the kitchen with a running buddy. She was prepping for a hundred-miler and needed to plan fuel for throughout her run. We tried a couple versions, and this was the winner. It's bright, fresh, filling, and fueling.

This recipe is portioned for 1 serving and most suited for adults.

Ingredients

- ¼ cup coconut milk
- 1 cup ice

- 2 clementines, peeled and segmented (you can use other oranges if you prefer, just aim for approximately 1½ cups)
- ½ cup mango, fresh or frozen
- 1 tsp ground turmeric
- 1 tsp ground ginger
- ½ Tbsp honey
- Vanilla protein powder (optional, for adults)
- 1 Tbsp maca powder (optional, for adults)

Directions

- Blend all ingredients until smooth.
- Ingredients like maca and protein make this more a Mama and Papa smoothie, but you can leave those ingredients out for younger palates.

Science: Turmeric contains the phenol curcumin, which has been found in clinical trials to decrease joint pain, decrease inflammation, and improve joint mobility and function after eight months of treatment. The spice has been found in studies to be protective for symptoms of sleep deprivation. Further, it's anti-inflammatory, antibacterial, and rich in antioxidants.

Green Mint Choco Chip Smoothie

Mint chocolate chip ice cream was my Friday afternoon treat from Laura Secord from the local mall when I was a child and teen (okay, and adult when home visiting from university). This smoothie brings those fond memories back for me, but perhaps you have your own memories with this classic flavor combo from the 1980s and '90s:

Ingredients

- 1 avocado
- 2 Tbsp cocoa powder
- 2 scoops powdered greens blend
- ⅓ cup cacao nibs or chocolate chips
- 1 Tbsp honey
- 2 drops spearmint extract or essential oil (refer to manufacturer to confirm it's safe for consumption)
- 3 cups milk or milk alternative
- Ice (optional)

Directions

- Blend all ingredients except cacao nibs/chocolate chips until smooth.
- Toward the end of blending process, add the cacao nibs/chocolate chips and pulse until dispersed but not fully broken down.
- If not being consumed right away, put all ingredients other than the milk and ice in freezer bag; pull out and put in fridge night before consuming/blending.

Minty Fresh Green Smoothie

A smoothie that has my heart, being my favorite color and refreshing for all the senses in the morning. Not all kids like this vegetable-heavy smoothie, but it's worth a try. It's portioned for 3–4 servings, but cut in half if only two are enjoying.

Ingredients

- 5 cups coconut water
- 6 stalks kale
- 2 green apples
- 1 cucumber
- 1 cup mint leaves
- 6 dates, pitted
- 1 serving protein powder (optional, for adults)

Directions

- Blend all ingredients in blender until smooth.

Maca Maca Man

This maca root-infused smoothie is creamy and nutty. It offers up a punch of energy and flavor. It isn't just for men, but my husband loves his maca-infused beverages, and research supports its use among men.

Note: this is portioned for 1 serving and only suitable for adults.

Ingredients

- 1 Tbsp almond butter
- 1 Tbsp maca powder
- 1 Tbsp cocoa powder
- 1 frozen banana
- 1 cup milk or milk alternative
- Pinch of salt
- Ice (optional)

Directions

- Blend all ingredients until smooth.
- If not being consumed right away, put all ingredients other than the milk and ice in freezer bag; pull out and put in fridge night before consuming/blending.

Science: Preliminary research suggests that maca has the ability to modestly boost your libido. In one study, published in the journal *Andrologia*, researchers gave men aged twenty-one to fifty-six a placebo or 3 grams of maca per day. After eight weeks, the men taking maca saw a bump in their sexual desire compared to the group taking placebo pills.

Gingerbread Smoothie

Support your immune system as well as mental and physical energy levels with this gingerbread smoothie. While our family loves this smoothie as a festive treat around Christmas, we also have it all year round.

Ingredients

- 3 cups milk or milk alternative
- 2 tsp molasses
- 1 tsp ground ginger
- 1 tsp ground cinnamon
- ½ tsp ground nutmeg
- 2 tsp vanilla extract
- 3 small frozen bananas
- 1 cup oats

Directions

- Blend all ingredients until smooth.
- If not being consumed right away, put all ingredients other than the milk and ice in freezer bag; pull out and put in fridge night before consuming/blending.

Science: Blackstrap molasses is a mineral-rich sweetener that contains magnesium, which relaxes muscles and decreases cortisol. It's also a source of iron.

Unicorn Smoothie

Whether you just find yourself with some leftover smoothie once you've filled your family's cups, or you're wanting to get playful with the smoothie experience on summer vacation or at a child's birthday party or a brunch, the unicorn smoothie is worth a trot.

Directions

- If you have a small amount of smoothie left in a blender after filling your and your family's cups, just pour in a mason jar, seal, and refrigerate. If the smoothie contains avocado, be sure to add some lemon juice to keep the avocado from going bad.
- You can also make any smoothie recipe and make layers that are different colors by mixing in natural colorants like raspberry juice, pumpkin purée, cocoa powder, spirulina, turmeric, and more.
- Serve up the unicorn smoothie in a clear container. Mason jars are great, but clear plastic cups are probably wise as a birthday party or brunch with my younger smoothie aficionados.

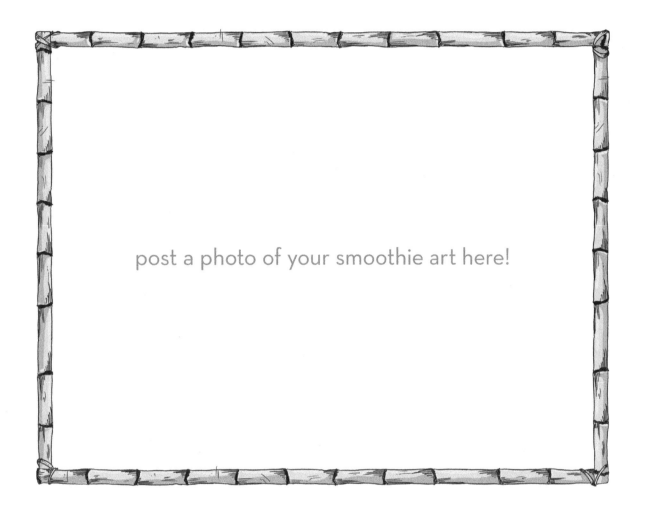

post a photo of your smoothie art here!

Eat and Drink: The Mindful Wino

• • • • • • • • • • • • • •

Wine tasting. It can be a mindful exercise and yet has traditionally been reserved for snobbery and pompous attitudes. At its core, wine tasting simply involves putting our own subjective sensations spurred by wine into words, and this leads to the impression of a wine lingering longer in our memory. Wine tasting experiences can help us communicate to other people what a particular wine is like, sometimes long after you've tasted it.

Ready to learn how to mindfully choose wine, including understanding the concepts of organic, biodynamic, and other wines; information about artificial additives; as well as mindfully tasting the wine with all the senses? I knew I'd get to put my wine and spirits training to use one of these days.

Mindful and Moderate

We are social creatures. Food and wine are a source of connecting with ourselves after a long day when we need a pause, with our partners, friends, extended family, and colleagues. That doesn't mean you have to partake in drinking and eating to be social. The message here is to be mindful of your choices, tapping into the senses, appreciating the moment to slow down.

Wine, in moderation, can have positive effects on your health. Numerous studies have shown so, from promoting longer life span to protecting against certain cancers, improving mental health, and benefiting the brain and heart.

Mindfully Preparing to Taste Wine

Tasting wine rather than simply drinking it increases our appreciation of the wine by allowing us to examine it in detail. Although the process can seem repetitive at first, with practice, it becomes a subconscious habit. Here are a few tips on how to taste your wine. Go about it with mindful awareness, not concerning yourself with whether others are judging you or if you're picking up the right flavor notes. Have fun; be playful.

Before tasting, cleanse the palate. Your tasting palate should be clean, unaffected by gum, coffee, toothpaste, food, and so on. Chewing a piece of bread can help remove lingering flavors. Also note: fatigue can impact your ability to judge wines because fatigue impacts your senses of smell and taste, and thus, your palate.

Mindful Wine Tasting Basics

1. **See.** Take time to look at the wine, leaning over it ever so slightly so that the wine spreads to the rim, and you can see its characteristics. This is best done over a white surface. Notice the color, opacity, and viscosity.

   - First check for haziness, which can be a fault of wine (but not always).
   - Is the color pale or intense?
   - What color is the wine? For a glass of red wine, is it purpley-red or orangey-red? For white wine, consider if it's yellow with hints of green or golden yellow. For rosé, is it bright purple-pink or brown?

2. **Swirl.** Swirl the glass for five to ten seconds to release the many aromas. You don't need to do this for every sip, just for the initial mindful wine tasting experience after pouring a glass.

3. **Smell.** Take a sniff. Identify at least two aromas from broad categories such as florals, fruits, vegetables, yeast (smells of bread or beer), wood, baking spices, coconut, smoke, or even pungent cardboard (which can indicate fault in a wine).

4. **Sip.** Take a small tasting sip. Then purse your lips like you have a straw between them and draw in air through your lips. This ensures the wine coats all parts of your mouth, and the vapors are carried up the back of your nose, where your sense of smell will detect the flavor characteristics.

5. **Savor.** Analyze the experience in your mouth: flavors (lemon, raspberry), structure (sweetness, alcohol, acidity, tannin), body (richness, weight, viscosity), and finish (how long wine flavors linger in the mouth after wine is swallowed or spat out; a long, complex finish is an indicator of quality).

6. **Subjective conclusion.** Ask yourself some questions:

   - Did I like this wine?
   - Did it seem balanced?
   - Was it unique?

Science: Unlike common belief and what we learned in grade school, all parts of the tongue are sensitive to all tastes. Thus, tasting is subjective and unique to everyone's palate. Certain areas of the tongue are more sensitive to some tastes than others; the exact pattern of sensitivities varies from person to person. In general, sweetness is most easily detected on the tip of the tongue, acidity on the sides, bitterness at the back.

Explore: Have a taste for wine tasting and want to dive a little deeper? Check out www.wsetglobal.com to learn about wine and spirit education available in your area and online.

Wine Pairing

The successful pairing of food with wine requires us to consider the separate components of the wine. Instead of merely going to specific food and wine pairings, let's cover a few basics. Knowing these basics will help you become more confident in wine and food pairing; you may even have the confidence to experiment with breaking the pairing rules.

- The wine should be sweeter than the food.
- The wine should be more acidic than the food (note: white, rosé, and sparkling wines tend to have more acidity).
- Red wines pair best with bold meats (red or game meat).
- White wines pair best with light-intensity meats (poultry) and fish.
- Bitter red wines are best balanced with fat (red meat, white cream, or butter sauces).
- Your best bet is to match the wine with the sauce rather than the meat.

Eat and Drink: Chia Pudding Parfait

Chia Pudding Parfait

Ingredients

- 2 cups buckwheat
- 2 cups maple cinnamon chia seed pudding (see recipe on page 208)
- 1 cup fresh or frozen berries
- ½ cup nuts and seeds
- Leftover smoothie (any flavor)

Directions

- In four 250 mL mason jars, layer with chia pudding, seeds, nuts, buckwheat seeds, leftover smoothie, frozen berries (if not being consumed right away; otherwise, use fresh berries).
- Get playful and mindful. Make it a piece of art that feeds your eye hunger for a more mindful and fun meal prep and eating experience.

Science: Cinnamon is a common spice these days, for good science-backed reason. When we lack sufficient rest (Oh, hello, all new parents), cinnamon attenuates insulin resistance and glucose intolerance observed following sleep loss. Cinnamon is also an antioxidant and anti-inflammatory, anti-diabetic, antimicrobial, and anticancer; it lowers lipids and cardiovascular disease, and it's reported to act against neurological disorders, such as Parkinson's and Alzheimer's diseases (Rao and Gan 2014).

Eat and Drink: The Mindful Art of the Smoothie Bowl

• • • • • • • • • • • • • • •

Smoothies are great in a glass, but bowls allow you to serve up an interactive eating experience. The creation of a smoothie bowl gives you a chance to play with your food, making a beautiful bowl that you and your children can feast on with your mouth and eyes (all the while engaging in the practice of mindful eating, whether you know it or not).

Ingredients

- 1–2 cups of any of the smoothie recipes in the previous section, but drop the amount of liquid slightly (depending on the recipe) to make for a thicker smoothie to hold up your nourishing toppings.
- Now it's time to choose your favorite toppings. The options are endless but can include the following:
    - Fresh fruit (sliced banana, pineapple, pear, peach; whole berries; cubed mango; grated apple)
    - Fresh vegetable (shredded carrot, beet)
    - Dried fruit (dehydrated apple, banana chips, cranberries, raisins, blueberries, golden berries, Incan berries)
    - Coconut (shredded or chips)
    - Cereal and granola
    - Nuts or nut butter
    - Honey or maple syrup
    - Protein powder
    - Herbs (rosemary, peppermint, spearmint, basil)
    - Spices (cinnamon, nutmeg, turmeric, ginger, cloves, vanilla bean, allspice, star anise, cardamom)
    - Seeds (hemp, chia, pumpkin, sesame, sunflower, fennel)
    - Dark chocolate (chopped bars, mini chips)
    - Cacao nibs

Directions

- Pour desired amount of smoothie into your bowl.
- If your smoothie is too thin to hold up your plethora of ingredients, try one of my hacks for thickening:
    - Use frozen berries, bananas, or zucchini when prepping your smoothie.
    - Stir in protein powder.
    - Add chia seeds and leave the smoothie bowl to sit in the fridge for a few minutes.
    - Put your bowl with smoothie in the freezer for five to ten minutes.
- Make an interesting design, from lines to mini mandalas, or create a picture like a field of flowers, a happy face, or more on your smoothie bowl.

Food is Joy

Eat and Drink: Bircher Muesli

• • • • • • • • • • • • • • •

Bircher muesli is a European classic that can help parents meal prep breakfasts for a few days at a time for the entire family. It's a recipe chock-full of protein, healthy fats, and carbs that can be customized to dietary restrictions and choosy taste buds.

Science: Oats are a whole grain that contains protein, fiber, manganese, phosphorous, vitamin B1, magnesium, chromium, and zinc. It can promote concentration, boost memory, and reduce stress.

I first encountered bircher muesli when I went on a four-month solo backpack trip across Europe as an undergrad. Many hostels just offered crisp rice cereal and a piece of fruit. There were a few with full spreads of European breakfasts, like the one I stayed at on Vondelpark in Amsterdam: sliced meats, cured fish, yogurt, cheese (ranging from fresh, soft, and spreadable to hard cheeses), bread baskets, pastries, fruits, veggies, and bircher muesli. Not the kind of breakfast you'd expect on a backpacking student's shoestring budget. Among the plethora of food I served myself up with (not entirely mindful of the space I had in my underfed belly) was the bircher muesli. And I've been hooked ever since.

Below is a base recipe for 1 serving. You can multiply the servings for multiple family members, or for meal prep for yourself for a few days.

Ingredients

- ½ cup rolled oats
- ¼ apple, chopped
- ¼ cup milk or milk alternative
- ¼ cup plain yogurt or yogurt substitute (such as dairy-free cultured coconut or cashew or soy yogurt)
- 1 Tbsp dried fruit (raisins, cranberries, blueberries, etc.)
- ¼ cup nuts, slivered or roughly chopped (almonds, walnuts, pecans, etc.)
- ½ Tbsp honey or maple syrup

Directions

- Add all ingredients to a mason jar or bowl.
- Combine well.
- Seal mason jar or bowl.
- Refrigerate at least twelve hours. Lasts a few days in the fridge, depending on yogurt due date and fruit ripeness.

Breaking the Basic Bircher

The best part of bircher muesli: You can get creative, and if you follow the basic recipe, it's pretty much fool-proof. Here are a few creative twists on the basic Bircher that the kids and I have come up with in the kitchen:

- **Visit the Tropics:** passionfruit and mango and pineapple and shredded coconut

- **Vanilla Berry:** blueberries and raspberries and blackberries and vanilla extract or seeds shaved from a fresh vanilla pod

- **Ch-Ch-Ch-Chia Cherry:** chia seeds and dried or fresh cherries (add slightly more liquid to the recipe, as chia seeds absorb a lot of liquid)

- **Chocolate-Covered Strawberries:** fresh strawberries and cacao nibs and unsweetened cocoa powder

- **Citrus Zing:** fresh orange segments and orange rind and walnuts and cinnamon and maple syrup to sweeten the base

- **PB&J:** peanut butter (sub in for some of the chopped nuts called for in the base) and fresh berries or jam (if using jam, we like to just add a dollop to the top of the bircher before refrigerating)

- **Choco-Nana:** banana and unsweetened cocoa powder

Eat and Drink: womlettes

• • • • • • • • • • • • • • •

I'm a lover of playing in the kitchen, food hacks, and plays on words, so this waffle-plus-omelette hybrid has me swooning. It's a brunch hack that has all the macros and is an easy way to cram in some veggies to nourish the brains and bodies of kiddos and parents. The waffle iron does all the work. And it's about time you put that wedding present gathering dust to good use.

Ingredients

- Oil or butter to grease waffle iron
- 5 eggs
- Dash of salt and pepper
- ⅓ cup milk (optional)

Directions

- Heat waffle iron (I use the large Belgian style, but any will do).
- Crack eggs in a small bowl and whisk. Whisk with milk if desired. Add any ingredients you want at this time (inspiration below).
- Pour egg mixture onto the waffle iron.
- Cook for 3–5 minutes. Like cooking a traditional omelette, you'll know it's done when it starts to brown and crisp.
- Carefully lift the womelette off the hot iron using a spatula and transfer to a plate.
- Top if you like (my personal favorite topping is a cheese and egg womelette with sliced avocado and sriracha).
- Womlettes can be made ahead and store in the fridge.

Womelette Inspiration

- **Gardener**: Omelette mix and smoked gouda and thyme and rosemary and chopped sundried tomatoes and garlic (topped with arugula)

- **Broccoli and Cheese**: Omelette mix and cheddar and broccoli and spinach

- **Farmer**: Omelette mix and ham and mushroom (topped with fresh dill)

- **Mediterranean**: Omelette mix and halved cherry tomatoes and olives and bell peppers and kale or spinach (topped with hummus)

- **Spanish**: Omelette mix and cooked chorizo sausage and black beans and Manchego cheese and green bell pepper (topped with salsa and sour cream)

History: The first written waffle recipe dates back to the fourteenth century, while the first omelette recipe dates back to the sixteenth century. The first womelettes featured on social media were circa 2016.

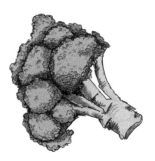

Science: Eggs are a complete protein source, and the yolks are high in choline. Choline is a precursor for acetylcholine, which is a neurotransmitter involved in memory.

Upgrade: Teach your kids to crack eggs, beat them, and add whatever they want for their womelettes. A womelette bar or dish with various womlettes can be a feature at a brunch with friends and family or for Christmas or Easter morning breakfast.

Eat: Mindful Meal Prep

Mindful eating is about more than just the act of eating your food; it's about meal planning, grocery list writing, shopping at local farmer's markets and grocery stores, and preparing the meal. Here you'll find quick tips on integrating mindful meal prep into your family's weekly ritual:

- **Get your child involved in food selection and meal prep.** Comfort foods are taking shape, and habits they develop now will stay with them for years after. Take your children grocery shopping and encourage them to select produce they want to try. As a family, make a habit of trying one different food, once a week. Children like to help; let them wash produce, set the table, toss the salad, sprinkle cheese or spices, or anything safe for their age. Make your children aware of the effort it takes to prepare a healthy meal; let them respect and understand the value of it.

- **Go for glass.** Use mason jars for food storage if meal prepping for meals on the go. Spillproof, and nontoxic to boot, you can toss them in your bag or suitcase and not worry about leakage (or about having to scramble, hangry, to find nourishing food on your travels or when on the go).

- **Identify your hunger.** As you wander into your pantry, open your desk drawer to grab a snack, pull up to the dinner table with your family, or are eating your kids' leftovers on their plates, take a moment to notice if you are experiencing a physical need or emotional desire that you're classifying as hunger. If emotional, notice the feelings that are coming up within you and what foods you're craving.

- **Declutter.** As you go to prepare a meal, take away distractions and clutter from the kitchen. This may mean washing the dirty dishes or clearing food prep surfaces. A clean kitchen will help you prepare your mindful meal.

- **Set the mood.** When you're about to do food prep or sit down for a meal, turn the TV off and put on music that relaxes you and assists in getting you to a more mindful place (for some, this may mean classical music; others may prefer acoustic rock). You can also diffuse essential oils and prepare a cup of herbal tea to comfort and relax you.

- **Breathe.** Before you prepare your food, take three deep breaths; in through your nose, out through your mouth. Likewise, before you eat, take three deep breaths; in through your nose, out through your mouth. This allows you to relax and feel more grounded. It also shifts your nervous system into a more restful state (parasympathetic nervous system), in which your mind can identify hunger types and levels better, and where you can better digest and receive maximum nutrition from your meal.

- **Consider the concept of division of responsibility.** Parents decide what to offer (healthy foods); when (mealtimes); where (in an environment supportive of feeding). Children decide if they are going to eat and how much.

- **Tap into your senses and get playful.** Food prep doesn't have to be a chore; get excited and really engage with your food. Both while you unpackage, wash, chop, slice, spiralize, blend, and mix your food, and while you eat. Look at your food; notice the colors. Notice the different scents your food offers. Take pause and look at the nourishing food in front of you. See the textures, flavors, macronutrients, and micronutrients. Tap into your inner kid, or observe your children eating to see how they squish, sniff, finely chop, and investigate their food. Also, as a parent, accept that each person is different and unique, including your child. There's no right or wrong way of eating; instead, there's a variety of ways and food experiences.

- **Make mealtimes for meals only.** While it's tempting to turn the TV on or feed your children when they are playing, try to avoid doing so. One of the principles of mindful eating is to direct all awareness to the feeding experience. Give them utensils and let them eat on their own (don't stress about the mess). At least once a day, eat meals together as a family. For younger kids, bring the high chair close to the table, or remove its tray and let your child use the family table.

- **Mindful foodie talk.** Parents can guide mindful eating conversations at the family table. Toddlers are learning colors, shapes, and textures, and food is the perfect teaching tool. During conversations, discuss what a healthy food is. They don't have big understanding of health, so start with basics. Instead of classifying food into good and bad, teach them to think of a healthy food as something that will help them grow, get tall, become strong, play more, or run fast.

- **Real talk regarding rewards.** Don't reward eating a healthy food with something unhealthy. "If you don't eat your vegetables, you can't have dessert." Yes, it's tempting, and I think we've all done it from time to time, but that type of statement implies they have to eat something nasty to get something sweet and delicious. This does not encourage your children to love eating vegetables. It also makes them attach happiness and success to unhealthy foods. Instead, make fruits and vegetables festive, reward with fun activities or special attention, and offer dessert occasionally, detached from eating any other food.

- **Take a mindful breath, and take it easy.** Let's be real: Your child won't eat the way you want all the time. Have an occasional treat, and allow your child to experiment with all foods. Most important of all, don't take the pleasure out of food. Create healthy eating memories, and at the same time, don't surrender or become a short-order cook. If they don't eat what you've offered for one meal, hunger will eventually kick in.

- **Give gratitude.** Give gratitude for all those who've had a hand in planting seeds, harvesting, taking care of animals, transporting your food to the market, and selling it in the grocery store. Don't forget yourself; practice gratitude for yourself for taking the time to gather nourishing foods to prepare to support your brain and body throughout the week. When it comes time to enjoy your meals throughout the week, be mindful to your body, expressing gratitude for its ability to receive a nourishing meal. This is an incredible lesson for kids as well that can start by taking them to the farmer's market to meet the farmers who have worked so hard to bring the food their parents serve them.

Eat and Drink: Maple Tahini Dressing

• • • • • • • • • • • • • • •

Maple tahini dressing has magical powers; it goes perfectly on almost any salad. If you are gluten-free, paleo, dairy-free, or vegan, this is a great option.

Ingredients

- ½ cup tahini
- 3 Tbsp maple syrup
- 2 tsp oil (coconut, olive, avocado, or grape seed)
- 3 tsp apple cider vinegar
- 1 juiced lemon
- Dash of salt and pepper
- 5 Tbsp hot water to thin

Directions

- Put all ingredients in a mason jar. Seal.
- Shake until combined.
- Store in fridge.

Eat and Drink: Green Mama and Papa Dressing

· · · · · · · · · · · · · · · · · ·

An upgraded version of the 1970s classic green goddess dressing that had mayonnaise for the first ingredient. This recipe is stacked with greens upon greens, from parsley to kale to lime to avocado.

Ingredients

- 1 avocado, skin removed and pitted
- 4 Tbsp lemon juice
- 2 cloves garlic, minced
- ½ cup fresh parsley
- 3 green onions
- 2 tsp sesame oil (or other oil)
- ½ tsp salt
- 4 dates, soaked in hot water for 5 minutes
- 1 tsp ginger, peeled and grated
- 1¼ cups water

Directions

- Place all ingredients in a food processor or blender.
- Blend until smooth.
- Serve as a dressing, marinade, or veggie dip, or as a sauce atop roasted veggies or meat.
- Store in airtight container in the fridge until ready to use for up to 1 week.

Science: You've likely seen all the buzz online and in local cafes featuring the healthy fat-filled fruit, avocado. The texture, nutrient density, and neutral flavor profile of avocados are just some of the reasons parents may want to think about having them in their families diets (if they don't already).

Eat and Drink: Golden Dressing

• • • • • • • • • • • • • • • •

This is a great recipe to dip raw veggies or baked chicken fingers in. Likewise, it makes for a great marinade for meat, tasty drizzle atop your Buddha bowl or salad bowl, or as the dressing base in your mason jar salad. It's an easy dressing for getting a dose of healthy fat from the olive oil and benefits from the anti-inflammatory duo of turmeric and black pepper.

Ingredients

- 2 Tbsp nutritional yeast
- 2 Tbsp honey
- ½ cup olive oil
- ½ cup apple cider vinegar or lemon juice
- 3 Tbsp Dijon mustard
- 1 tsp ground turmeric
- ½ tsp black pepper
- ½ tsp sea salt

Directions

- Combine all ingredients in a medium-sized mason jar fitted with a lid.
- Shake until combined.
- Store in airtight container in the fridge until ready to use for up to 1 week. Shake jar before each use.

Eat and Drink: Modern Mushy Peas

• • • • • • • • • • • • • • • •

With family from the UK, I had my fair share of mushy peas growing up. It's truly a comfort food for me, and one of the first foods I served to my babies … with a little brainy upgrade. Peas don't get much attention on food blogs and Instagram, but they are little nutritional powerhouses.

Ingredients

- ½ cup peas (fresh or frozen)
- 1 avocado, cubed
- Juice of ½ a lemon
- Dash of salt

Directions

- If using frozen peas, thaw in a bowl of warm water, drain off any excess water.
- Put all ingredients in a food processor.
- Process until well combined and smooth.
- Store in the fridge in a sealed container. Ensure the container is small, with limited space at the top. Lemon juice keeps it from browning.
- Serve on its own as a main dish for a baby, a side dish, or a dip for veggies or crackers. You can also use this Modern Mushy Peas recipe to switch up your morning avocado toast by smearing it atop your favorite bread (it's delish with sourdough; check out avocado toast recipes for inspiration on page 189). More usages include adding a spoonful to a Buddha bowl or salad.

Upgrade: I like to mix in a powdered greens blend when feeling the need for more nutrients in this recipe. Always check the ingredients and usage on your powdered greens to ensure they are suitable for your age and any health conditions.

Science: Peas are a legume, belonging to the same family as soy beans, kidney beans, lentils, and chickpeas. Legumes are an eco-friendly food that help deposit nitrogen in our soils. Peas are high in beta-carotene, iron, and protein.

Eat and Drink: Batch-Cooked Roasted Veggies

• • • • • • • • • • • • • •

Parents, if you're going to roast veggies, you may as well roast a large batch.

Ingredients

- 1 head of cauliflower (or bag of precut florets)
- 3 large sweet potatoes sliced into round slices
- 20 baby potatoes, halved
- 15 brussels sprouts, stemmed
- 3 bell peppers, chopped
- ½ onion, diced
- 2 Tbsp olive oil
- Dash of sea salt

Directions

- Preheat oven to 425°F
- Line 2 baking sheets with parchment paper.
- Toss veggies and seasoning in a large bowl until evenly coated.
- Spread veggies on baking sheets.
- Bake for 45 minutes. Stir/shake pan one to two times during cooking.

Upgrade: Curious how to use these roasted veggies? You can serve as a dinner side dish, scramble with eggs, put in a salad, top a Buddha bowl, purée into a dip, incorporate into a soup.

Eat and Drink: Avocado 101 and Avocado Toast

• • • • • • • • • • • • •

Avocado is the pear-shaped fruit, a nutritional powerhouse with a nutty taste and buttery texture. While it may be a fad food featured all over social media and on food blogs, it offers up a variety of uses, and it's nutrient dense.

> **Science**: Avocados are a great source of mono-unsaturated fatty acids (helps to lower LDL, or bad cholesterol, and increase HDL, or good cholesterol); vitamins A, E, and K; iron, copper, magnesium, and manganese; as well as dietary fiber.

Shopping for and Storing Avocados

Curious how to pick the best avocados? If you want to consume right away, the fruit should yield slightly when light pressure is applied (gently press with fingertips). Avocados that are hard will require quite a few days to ripen. Avocados that are overripe will feel mushy to touch. Skin color can range from lighter green to dark green, almost black. Avoid fruits with dark blemishes, indentations, or punctured skin.

How you store your avocado depends on both its ripeness and when you want to use it. Store in the fridge to slow the ripening process. Store at room temperature near apples or bananas to speed up the ripening process.

Ways to Use Avocado

One of the reasons I love this fruit is that there are so many uses for various taste buds and meals.

- **Bake with it.** You can substitute avocado for butter in a 1:1 ratio. To do this, scoop out the avocado and press the pulp into a measuring cup (you may need to increase your wet ingredients to compensate).

- **Smash and smear it.** Smash and cream an avocado with a fork. Then smear on toast, bagel, or apple slices as a tasty alternative to other spreads like cream cheese.

- **Blend it.** Throw an avocado into the blender with your other fave smoothie ingredients. It adds a nice creamy texture and rich nutty flavor.

- **Purée it.** Avocados add flavor to any soup. They can be used in hot or chilled soups (such as hot chicken and lime avocado soup or chilled cucumber and avocado soup).

- **Slice it.** Use avocados as a salad topper for a boost of color and nutrition.

- **Cream it.** Use avocados as a mayo substitute for egg salad, chicken salad, or tuna salad sandwiches.

Avocado Toast Recipes

Here are a few recipes for avocado toast. Just smash and smear your avocado and add the toppings of your choice below. Note that you can use any type of bread, from sourdough to gluten free, as well as rye crisp breads, baked sweet potato slices, rice cakes, and more. Add your own creative energy.

- **Good Morning:** avocado and sliced hard-boiled egg/pickled egg/over-easy egg and chili flakes and salt

- **Spicy:** avocado and corn and black beans and salsa and lime juice and paprika

- **Sweet:** avocado and cinnamon and cocoa nibs and honey

- **Fresh:** avocado and feta and mint and shaved or sliced cucumber

- **Fall Foodie:** avocado and cinnamon and walnuts and sliced pear and crumbled Gorgonzola cheese and honey

- **Sweet Pea:** Modern Mushy Peas (see recipe on page 186)

post a photo of your avocado art here!

Eat and Drink: Baked Chicken Two Ways

• • • • • • • • • • • • • •

Eating the same flavor day in and day out will have your taste buds fatiguing. So try these two simple marinades for one tray or bag of chicken. Note: you can use these marinades with other meats or cubed tofu; just adjust cooking time accordingly.

Sweet and Smokey Chicken Marinade Ingredients

- ½ tray chicken thighs or breasts, cubed
- 1 lemon, juiced
- 2 Tbsp honey
- 2–3 tsp mild paprika
- 1 tsp ground turmeric
- 1 tsp ground ginger

Herb Chicken Marinade Ingredients

- ½ tray chicken thighs or breasts, cubed
- Handful of fresh herbs, chopped (your preference: thyme, rosemary, parsley, sage, oregano, marjoram)
- 2 Tbsp olive oil
- Dash of salt

Directions

- Put each marinade in separate bags. Toss to coat chicken. Can cook immediately or allow to marinate in fridge overnight.
- Preheat oven to 450°F.
- Use tinfoil to cover and separate two sides of a baking sheet. Or prepare on two baking sheets.
- Split between the two sides or trays. Pour dressing over each side.
- Cook for 25–30 minutes. Turn/toss chicken halfway through cooking.

Eat and Drink: Baked Chickpeas Two Ways

• • • • • • • • • • • • • • • • •

Baked chickpeas are a satisfying and nutrient-dense snack on their own, as nutritious "croutons" on a salad, or a topping for a rice dish or Buddha bowl.

Cheesy Chickpea Ingredients

- 1 can chickpeas, drained and rinsed
- 1 Tbsp olive oil
- 2 Tbsp nutritional yeast
- 1 tsp paprika
- Salt and pepper to taste

Curry Chickpea Ingredients

- 1 can chickpeas, drained and rinsed
- 2 Tbsp melted coconut oil
- 2 tsp curry powder
- 1 tsp turmeric
- 1 tsp salt

Directions

- Preheat oven to 400°F.
- Use tinfoil to cover and separate two sides of a baking sheet. Or prepare on two baking sheets and cover with parchment paper.
- Rinse chickpeas. Dry by rolling between paper towel or kitchen towel.
- Transfer to large bowl.
- Add remaining ingredients and stir to coat.
- Transfer chickpeas to baking sheet(s).
- Roast for 30 minutes or until golden and crispy. Toss chickpeas halfway through cooking.
- Enjoy immediately or store in an airtight container for up to a week.

Upgrade: You can also choose to sub in pinto beans, black beans, or peas for chickpeas in these recipes.

Eat and Drink: The Art of the Buddha Bowl

• • • • • • • • • • • • • • •

Buddha bowl. Glory bowl. Hippie bowl. Whatever the name, the nourishing value is full on. When people use the words "Buddha bowl," it's often to describe a deep bowl overflowing with vibrant food. Buddha bowls are hearty dishes made of greens, raw or roasted veggies, legumes, spices, grains and pseudo-grains, nuts, seeds, and dressing. Full of texture, color, scents and flavor, it's tough *not* eating these bowls mindfully. The Buddha bowl is traditionally a vegan bowl, but eating mindfully means listening to your body, your cravings, and not so much to your mind, which may be labeling food "good" or "bad."

Why Have a Buddha Bowl?

First, the research is overwhelming when it comes to encouraging plants in your diet, and plant-based protein is not only good for the mind and body, but also the environment. Further, making meals that are beautiful will support you and your family in taking pause and appreciating food you nourish with. Feasting with the eyes is a great way to integrate more mindful eating habits into your life, which has the potential to reduce picky eating, craving-related eating, and emotional eating, as well as support healthy weight management.

How to Make a Buddha Bowl

Ready to make some #foodart? Roll up your sleeves, turn on some good-vibe music, take a few deep breaths, grab a deep bowl, and get ready for some nourishment. For Buddha bowls, the tradition is to make a vegan dish with grains at the bottom, artful array of colorful roasted and raw veggies/fruit, as well as protein of choice and greens, a drizzle of homemade dressing, and sprinkling of seeds or nuts on top.

Before you eat, take a moment to allow your eyes to feast on the bounty of nourishing plant-based food before you. Take ten deep breaths. Mindful eating means learning to attend to our body's hungry and fullness cues. So assess how hungry you are on a scale of 0 to 10 (10 being overstuffed); check in with your level of hunger midway through and toward the end of the meal. There's no award for joining the clean plate club, even works of art like Buddha bowls. The contents of these bowls are great for leftovers.

Buddha
build your own Bowl

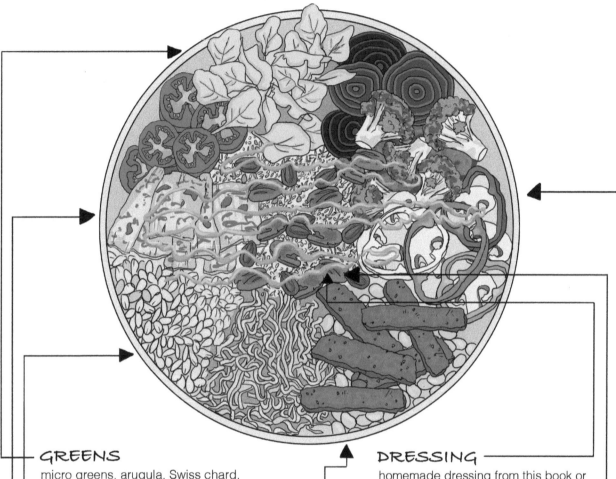

GREENS
micro greens, arugula, Swiss chard, massaged kale, spinach, romaine, cilantro, parsley, basil

FERMENTS
pickled veg, kimchi, kraut

GRAINS
rice, quinoa, barley, buckwheat, couscous, farro, ramen noodles

PROTEIN
tofu, tempeh, black beans, pinto beans, edamame, chickpeas

DRESSING
homemade dressing from this book or store bought

TOPPINGS
almonds, pine nuts, walnuts, pecans, hemp hearts, sesame seeds, pumpkin seeds, chia seeds, nutritional yeast, dulse flakes

ROAST OR RAW VEG
radishes, beets, onions, corn, celery, carrots, bell peppers, zucchini, avocado, tomato, cucumber, mushrooms, broccoli, peas, olives, sweet potato

Buddha Bowl Recipe

Recipe is for 1 serving, or 2 child servings.

Ingredients

- ½ cup grains or pseudo-grains (quinoa, rice, buckwheat, etc.)
- ½ cup protein (roasted chickpeas or chicken)
- 1 cup roasted or fresh vegetables
- 1–2 Tbsp seeds or nuts (pine nuts, sesame seeds, almonds, cashews, chia seeds, etc.)
- 1 cup greens (spinach, kale, arugula, etc.)
- 1–2 Tbsp dressing (for homemade recipe ideas, check out pages 183-185)

Directions

- Put grains at the base of bowl, artfully arrange other ingredients on top or around, then drizzle desired dressing on top.

- This is also a fun activity for kids. Just scale down the size of bowl and ingredients for baby Buddha bowls.

Eat and Drink: The Art of the Mason Jar Salad

• • • • • • • • • • • • • • •

Mason jar salads are basically Buddha bowls transferred into clear mason jars for easy transport (and not to mention eye appeal).

Science: You can reduce your family's environmental footprint and toxic load, as well as have nourishing food on the go, by reusing glass jars instead of storing your salad in a plastic container. Research I've been involved with has shown that BPA and phthalate exposure impact the cognitive development of preschoolers.

Explore: Check out your kitchen's food storage container drawer or cupboard (cue avalanche of plastic lids and bottoms, none of which are matching). Consider replacing some or all with glass containers, whether purchased specifically for food storage or recycled glass pasta sauce or baby food jars.

build your own salad jar

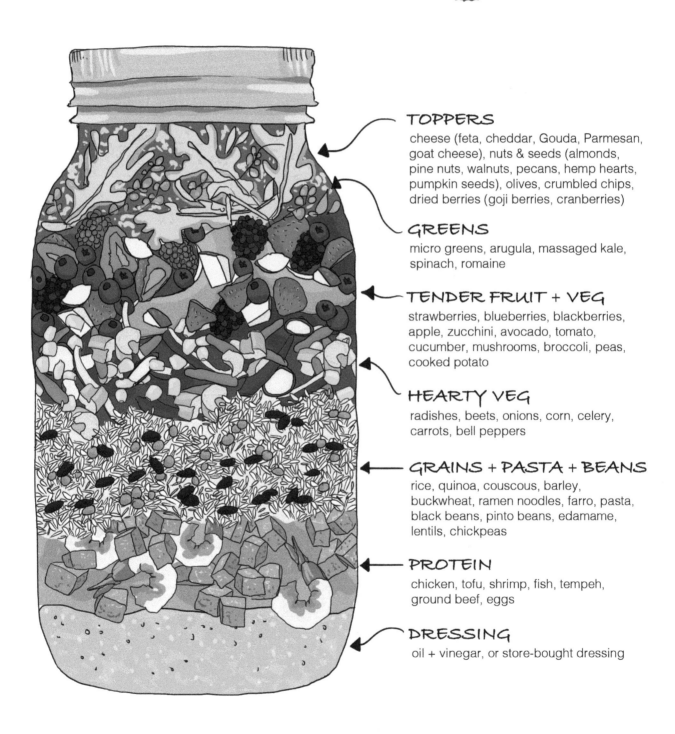

TOPPERS
cheese (feta, cheddar, Gouda, Parmesan, goat cheese), nuts & seeds (almonds, pine nuts, walnuts, pecans, hemp hearts, pumpkin seeds), olives, crumbled chips, dried berries (goji berries, cranberries)

GREENS
micro greens, arugula, massaged kale, spinach, romaine

TENDER FRUIT + VEG
strawberries, blueberries, blackberries, apple, zucchini, avocado, tomato, cucumber, mushrooms, broccoli, peas, cooked potato

HEARTY VEG
radishes, beets, onions, corn, celery, carrots, bell peppers

GRAINS + PASTA + BEANS
rice, quinoa, couscous, barley, buckwheat, ramen noodles, farro, pasta, black beans, pinto beans, edamame, lentils, chickpeas

PROTEIN
chicken, tofu, shrimp, fish, tempeh, ground beef, eggs

DRESSING
oil + vinegar, or store-bought dressing

Eat and Drink: Quinoa Cobb Salad

• • • • • • • • • • • • • •

This savory and sweet quinoa salad is an ode to the Cobb salad. Recipe is for 1 teen/adult serving or 2 child servings.

Ingredients

- ½ cup cooked quinoa
- ½ cup cubed herbed chicken
- 1 cup roasted vegetables
- 1 hard-boiled egg, peeled and sliced
- 5 cherry tomatoes
- Fresh dill
- 1 cup massaged kale (or other preferred greens)
- ⅓ cup cheesy roasted chickpeas (on page 191)
- 2 Tbsp golden dressing (on page 185)

Directions

- Choose to serve in (1) bowl or (2) mason jar to go.
- For (1), put greens at the base of bowl, artfully arrange other ingredients on greens, then drizzle golden dressing on top; top with cheesy roasted chickpeas.
- For (2), put 2 Tbsp golden dressing at the base of the mason jar, put all ingredients in the mason jar, going in order for the salad ingredients (so the chickpeas are at the top).

Science: Quinoa is considered a complete protein because it contains all eight essential amino acids as well as high levels of calcium, phosphorous, iron, and B vitamins. In addition, quinoa supplies valuable starch and fiber to the diet.

Eat and Drink: Mindful of Your Snack Time

Here's an array of quick-to-prep snacks that satisfy stomach hunger and are attractive enough for the eyes to feast on.

Stuffed Dates

- Pit and open 3 dates.
- Fill each date with 1 tsp nut butter.
- Top with a sprinkle of chia seeds, hemp seeds, or crumbled dark chocolate.

Apple with Chia Pudding Dip

- Slice 1 apple into strips or large slices.
- Dip into the maple cinnamon chia pudding (refer to recipe on page 208)

Hummus and Veggies/Crackers

- Scoop ½ cup hummus (store-bought or use the recipe on page 202) into a bowl or put at the bottom of a mason jar.
- Have veggies (carrots, cucumber, zucchini, tomato, etc.) cut into stick shapes arranged on a plate or dipped into the mason jar and seal with a lid if it's a snack for on-the-go.

Hard-Boiled Egg

- Place eggs in a saucepan in a single layer, add cold water to cover, heat water over high heat until boiling.
- Remove from burner, cover pan, and let eggs stand for 12 minutes.
- Drain immediately.
- Peel and serve.

  Upgrade 1: Season with fresh or dried dill and paprika and sea salt
  Upgrade 2: Serve with dip: honey mustard, Dijon mustard, or hummus
  Upgrade 3: For a more substantial snack, serve with a half-slice organic whole grain bread or a few whole grain or gluten-free crackers.

Apple Sandwiches

- Slice 1 apple.
- Spread 1 Tbsp nut butter between apple slices.

Cheesy Popcorn

- Either freshly pop or buy organic popcorn.
- In a large bowl, serve 4 cups popcorn.
- Add ½ Tbsp melted grass-fed butter or olive oil and 1 Tbsp nutritional yeast and dash of salt.

Banana Pop

- Peel 2 organic bananas.
- Place on a large skewer or popsicle stick.
- Dip in nutty chocolate mix (⅓ cup melted chocolate and 1 Tbsp nut butter).
- Sprinkle with coconut, wrap in cling wrap, and freeze.
- Pull out 5–10 minutes before eating.

Fruit Kabobs and Dip

- Get 4 sticks suitable for kabobs.
- Place cubed or whole fruits to put on kabob (whole strawberries, sliced bananas, cubed mango, cubed melon, pineapple chunks, etc.).
- Dip the kabob sticks in yogurt seasoned with 1 tsp of cinnamon.

Trail Mix

- Check out the playful trail mix inspiration on page 200-201. Fill a small glass jar to take with you on the go in your bag, in a backpack, or in your vehicle.

Eat and Drink: Choose Your Own Trail Mix Adventure

· · · · · · · · · · · · ·

Today you can find trail mixes everywhere from small speciality healthy stores to big box stores. They're a good option on the go, but you can skip the preservatives and packages and seize the opportunity to get yourself or your kids involved in making (and eating) a custom-made snack. From sweet to savory, crunchy to chewy, there are thousands of combinations to appeal to any age and palate. Kids and parents alike will get a fun surprise in every bite.

> **History**: One of the earliest written records of trail mix was in camping guides written by outdoorsman and American travel writer Horace Kephart, circa 1910 (Kephart 1916). His recipe included nuts, raisins, and chocolate. The intention of this first trail mix—a combination of nuts and raisins—was for it to be eaten while being active outdoors.

Trail mix is lightweight, portable, and full of energy-dense ingredients that cover all the macros: fat, carbs, protein. Simply combine any dry ingredients and stash the mix in an airtight container, then you're good to go—on the trail or out and about in town. A staple in my Volvo, picnic basket, diaper bag, gym bag, in-flight bag, or road trip cooler; all contain jars of ever-rotating trail mix ingredients.

Choose Your Own Adventure Trail Mix Ingredients

Nuts (almonds, pistachios, cashews, peanuts, walnuts, hazelnuts, Brazil nuts, pecans, pine nuts)

Seeds (pumpkin, sunflower, sesame, flax, hemp seeds)

Dried fruit (apples, cherries, cranberries, goji berries, blueberries, strawberries, apricots, raisins, bananas, figs, pineapple chunks, mango, dates)

Dried veggies (kale chips, dried beet chips, seaweed chips, wasabi peas, candied ginger)

Grains (cereal, pretzels, crackers, granola, popcorn, graham crackers, puffed rice, fish crackers, broken tortilla chips, sesame sticks)

Sweets (chocolate chips/chunks, peanut butter chips, butterscotch chips, cacao nibs, mini marshmallows, gummies, yogurt-covered raisins or pretzels, chocolate-covered coffee beans)

Savory snacks (wasabi peas, dried ginger)

Spices and herbs (dash of ground cinnamon, ginger, nutmeg, garlic, sea salt, cardamom, chili, curry mix, lucuma, cocoa, mesquite, rosemary)

Themed Trail Mix Ingredients

- **Gone Fishin'**: fish crackers and pine nuts and kale chips
- **It's a Zoo in Here**: animal crackers and raisins and peanuts and popcorn
- **Chocolate-Covered Cherries**: dried cherries and chocolate chips/chunks and Brazil nuts and macadamia nuts
- **Berry-Licious**: dried berries (choose favorites from golden berries, mulberries, strawberries, goji berries, blueberries, cranberries) and sunflower seeds and pistachios
- **S'more Fun**: mini marshmallows and chocolate chips/chunks and graham crackers broken to pieces (or Teddy Grahams) and peanuts
- **Sea Snacks**: wasabi peas and seaweed pieces/crackers and sesame sticks and puffed rice and peanuts
- **Orchard Picking**: chopped dried apricots and dried apples and cashews and pecans
- **Seaside Adventure**: salted pretzels and fish gummies and almonds
- **Taco 'Bout a Mix**: broken tortilla chips and dash each of paprika and garlic powder (or taco seasoning) and cashew nuts and fish crackers
- **Hawaiian Paradise**: cashews and macadamia nuts and dried pineapple and dried mango chunks and large coconut chips
- **Fall Harvest**: candied pecans and pumpkin seeds and dried cranberries and cereal
- **Apple Pie**: walnuts and almonds and dried apple chunks or chips and chopped dates and dash of lucuma powder and dash of cinnamon
- **Gingerbread House**: candied ginger chunks and raisins and hazelnuts and granola clusters and dash of nutmeg and cinnamon
- **Banana Split**: dried bananas and dried strawberries and chocolate chips/chunks and peanuts

Trail Mix Directions

- Choose a suggested themed recipe above or create your own trail adventure. For your own adventure, you can choose an ingredient or two from each or combine a couple of the categories.
- Store in an airtight container such as a large or small mason jar.
- Keep your trail mix in a dry, cool place. If you are like me and keep a mason jar of trail mix in your vehicle and running stroller at all times, be mindful of not adding candy chips and other ingredients that can melt in warmer months.
- Happy trails (mix) to you.

Upgrade: For your first bite, choose one morsel from your trail mix. You can do this with a friend, partner, child, or solo. Do the Mindful Breathing and Eating Meditation Practice found earlier in this section (on page 150).

Eat and Drink: Humble Hummus

• • • • • • • • • • • • • •

A simple hummus can be made with your preferred beans, spices, and oil, along with tahini and lemon juice. Liven up the taste buds by switching up the flavor with each batch. My current favorite is cumin and chipotle with black beans.

Ingredients

- 1 small can of beans (garbanzo, navy, black, black-eyed, lima, etc.)
- 2 Tbsp oil (olive, avocado, etc.)
- Juice of ½ lemon
- 4 Tbsp tahini
- Pinch of salt
- Spices (optional; paprika, chipotle, ground truffle, cumin, coriander)
- Herbs (optional; dill, parsley, cilantro, basil)

Directions

- Combine all ingredients in food processor.
- Process until well combined and smooth.

Eat and Drink: Friyay Family Charcuterie

· · · · · · · · · · · · · ·

How times have changed: From after-work drinks with coworkers and getting lost in the flow of conversation, to the desire in the now to connect with one's family at the end of the week. Charcuteries cut down food prep time, are a fun foodie art activity kids can help prepare, and are a chance for kids to lead the way in choosing what they want to eat.

Below are categories and ingredients you can consider for your Friyay Family Charcuterie. Then mindfully arrange on a large board or a couple smaller boards, whatever you have at your disposal.

Meat and Cheese

This is one of my favorite parts of the charcuterie. I take my oldest to a local cheese shop most Fridays, and he gets to pick a new cheese we've never tried before. Then we hit a deli for some meat.

- hard cheese
- soft or spreadable cheese
- nondairy cheese (such as fermented cashew cheese or soy-based cheese)
- sliced sausage
- sliced deli meat

Bread and Crackers

Variety is key.

- sliced sourdough
- toasted baguette
- grain crackers
- gluten-free crackers

Dips

- veggie purée, made from the roasted veggies (page 187)
- Humble Hummus (page 202) or store-bought hummus
- guacamole
- Modern Mushy Peas (page 186)
- spinach dip

Condiments

- honey
- mustard

- fig jam
- red pepper jelly
- pickles

Fruits and Veggies

- sliced bell peppers
- sliced fresh apples or dehydrated apples
- grapes
- blueberries
- dried apricots
- olives

Wine and Juice Pairing

Take some of the principles from the Mindful Wino Piece in this book (pages 172-173) to pair wines and juices with your featured ingredients on the charcuterie.

- sparkling fruit drinks
- grape juice
- apple juice
- pomegranate juice
- lemonade
- nonalcoholic ginger beer
- red wine
- rosé wine
- white wine
- sparkling wine

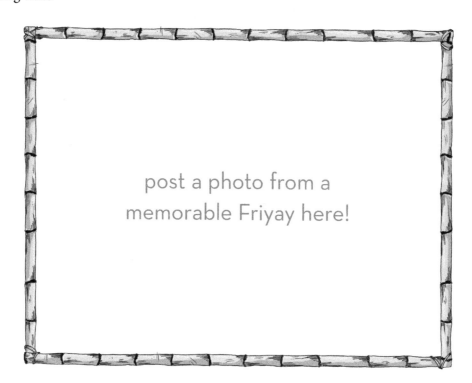

post a photo from a memorable Friyay here!

Eat and Drink: Interactive Popcorn Bar

• • • • • • • • • • • • • • • •

Try this interactive popcorn bar for your next family movie night, a sleepover your child's hosting, or get-togethers with adult friends.

Homemade Popcorn Topping Blends

Mindfully thought out, including these fun superfood flavorings:

- **Nacho Cheese**: paprika and nutritional yeast and sea salt
- **Deep Sea:** seaweed and spirulina and nutritional yeast
- **Salted Caramel**: lucuma (a ground fruit that tastes like caramel) and sea salt
- **Caramel Apple:** lucuma and cinnamon and dehydrated apples

Popcorn Service

Here are a few of our family's favorite ways to serve up popcorn, whether for a family movie night, a birthday party sleepover, or movie date with other families:

- paper bags with markers for each person to doodle name or designs
- mason jars
- reusable nonbreakable bowls for young kids

Science: There's interesting research by Dr. Brian Wansink, who runs the Food and Brand Lab at Cornell University. He explored how people mindlessly eat popcorn in movies. In terms of quantity, he found that people ate 34–45 percent more popcorn out of big buckets than medium-sized buckets. He believes large portions suggest larger consumption norms. Dr. Wansink also found that people watching sad movies eat more, possibly to compensate for sadness. Those watching adventure movies tend to eat more as the pace of the movie increased. Dr. Wansink's advice for not overeating while watching a movie? Make appropriate portions per person or keep food out of reach during a movie.

Explore: If you haven't tried lucuma, the flavor is similar to caramel but it's actually a ground-down fruit. You can purchase it at most health food stores. Nutritional yeast has a cheesy flavor that is used for many vegan "cheese" dishes like vegan mac and cheese. You can buy at most health food stores.

Eat and Drink: Dehydrated Ginger Snap Cookies

• • • • • • • • • • • • • •

A few years back, I stayed at Jan Chozen Bays's Great Vow Zen Monastery, completing training in the Mindful Eating Conscious Living Program. While there, I got friendly and volunteered time with the residents on rotation in the kitchen. One of said residents wanted to make use of all the leftover nut pulp instead of sending it all to the garbage or compost. This cookie recipe is inspired by her. These are great treats for teatime or recess for all ages, and they also make a great gift during the holidays.

Ingredients

- 2 cups almond pulp (well drained but still moist)
- ¾ cup dried shredded coconut
- ⅓ cup maple syrup
- 1 tsp ground ginger, or 2 tsp grated fresh ginger
- 1 tsp cinnamon
- 1 Tbsp blackstrap molasses
- 1 tsp vanilla
- Dash of salt

Directions

- Place all ingredients in a large bowl.
- Combine ingredients.
- Form into small cookies.
- Place cookies on dehydrator tray or parchment paper. Dehydrate on high for 1 hour. Reduce temperature to 105 degrees and dehydrate until crispy (approximately 6 hours).

Eat and Drink: Peanut Butter Cookie Dough Bites

• • • • • • • • • • • • •

This is a great recipe for getting young kids helping and engaged in the kitchen. Allow time to tidy up the mess after and prep your child for their responsibilities for cleaning post-cookie making. This recipe makes a dozen cookies.

Ingredients

- ½ cup quick oats
- ½ cup almond meal/ground almonds
- ½ cup shredded coconut
- 2 Tbsp cacao nibs
- 2 Tbsp peanut butter
- 1 Tbsp maca powder
- 1 Tbsp honey
- Pinch of vanilla powder

Directions

- Place all ingredients in a bowl and mix until combined.
- Roll into balls and store in the fridge or freezer.

Eat and Drink: Maple Cinnamon Chia Pudding

• • • • • • • • • • • • • • •

You've likely seen chia pudding at cafes and health food stores. It's a filling snack that most ages can enjoy. It's also flexible with flavor, as chia seeds don't have a strong flavor. Consider the prep of chia pudding as being part of your child's weekly chores.

Upgrade: Adults can add protein powder to the chia pudding recipe featured in this book for a quick post-workout treat.

Science: Chia seeds, which come in white or black seeds, are a great source of healthy omega-3, calcium, manganese, phosphorus, and fiber. They also have been reported to stabilize blood sugar, boost energy, and aid in digestion. Dates contain calcium, iron, phosphorus, sodium, potassium, magnesium, zinc, vitamin A, and vitamin K, and they are a good source of fiber. They have been reported to boost energy, improve digestive functioning, and relieve constipation.

Ingredients

- ⅔ cup chia seeds
- 2 tsp cinnamon
- 3 cups milk or milk alternative
- 4 Tbsp maple syrup

Directions

- Mix all ingredients and leave to sit for 10 minutes.
- Store again and scrape edges so chia seed clumps are not exposed to liquid.
- Store in fridge for 5+ hours until chia seeds have soaked up all the liquid. Can be stored for a week.

Eat and Drink: Choco-Cado Mousse

• • • • • • • • • • • • • •

Here's a five-ingredient mousse that can be made in a blender in 2 minutes.

Ingredients

- 2 avocados
- ½ cup unsweetened cocoa powder
- 2 Tbsp honey
- ¼ cup nut milk (or other milk preference)
- 2 tsp vanilla extract

Directions

- Blend all ingredients in blender or food processor until smooth.
- Refrigerate pudding until chilled, about 30 minutes.

Upgrade: Looking for a dessert for a special dinner or birthday party? Parents and kids can make mousse cups in cute cups or small mason jars. Try topping the mousse with crumbled cookies and gummy worms, fun for a summer or kids' party. Or layer sliced bananas or strawberries.

Eat and Drink: Nice Cream

• • • • • • • • • • • • • • • •

"Ice cream" can be made of frozen organic bananas and vegetables in your blender. Parents can get creative and add spices or other fruits to the mix. These recipes are for approximately 4 to 5 servings.

Banana Bread Nice Cream

Ingredients

- 4 bananas, frozen
- ½ cup walnuts, ideally sprouted
- ¼ cup cacao nibs
- ¼ cup ground flax seed
- 1 tsp cinnamon

Directions

- Soak walnuts for about 12 hours.
- Peel and freeze bananas.
- Remove bananas from freezer. Allow to sit for about 30–45 minutes before prepping recipe.
- Place bananas in a food processor or blender. You may add almond milk or other liquid to assist in blending.
- Pulse or blend until smooth and creamy.
- Add the walnuts, cacao nibs, flax seed, and cinnamon to the banana cream.
- Pulse to combine ingredients. Make sure not to overdo it, as you want the cacao nibs to be like chocolate chip chunks in the nice cream.

Berry Nice Cream

Ingredients

- 4 large frozen bananas
- 1 cup frozen berries
- 1 cup coconut cream

Directions

Process all ingredients in a blender until smooth.

Upgrade: Adults can add some protein powder into these nice creams after a strenuous workout or run outside.

References

Altmaier, E., and R. Maloney. 2007. "An Initial Evaluation of a Mindful Parenting Program." *Journal of Clinical Psychology* 63:1231–1238. doi: 10.1002/jclp.20395.

Arumugam, M., et al. 2011. "Enterotypes of the Human Gut Microbiome." *Nature* May 12;473(7346):174–80.

Baker-Ericzen, M. J., L. Brookman-Frazee, and A. Stahmen. 2005. "Stress Levels and Adaptability in Parents of Children with and without Autism-Spectrum Disorder." *Research & Practice for Persons with Severe Developmental Disabilities.* 30:194–204. doi: 10.2511/rpsd.30.4.194.

Barnes, S., K. W. Warren-Brown, E. Krusemark, and W. K. Campbell. 2007. "The Role of Mindfulness in Romantic Relationship Satisfaction and Responses to Relationship Stress." *Journal of Marital and Family Therapy* 33:482–500. doi: 10.1111/j.1752-0606.2007.00033.x.

Bögels, S. M., and M. Brechman-Toussaint. 2006. "Family Factors in the Aetiology and Maintenance of Childhood Anxiety: Attachment, Family Functioning, Rearing, and Parental Cognitive Biases." *Clinical Psychology Review* 26:834–856. doi: 10.1016/j.cpr.2005.08.001.

Bögels, S. M., G. Sijbers, and M. Voncken. 2006. "Mindfulness- and Task-Concentration Training for Generalized Social Phobia." *Journal of Cognitive Psychotherapy* 20:33–44. doi: 10.1891/jcop.20.1.33.

Bögels, S. M., B. Hoogstad, L. Dun, S. Schutter, and K. Restifo. 2008. "Mindfulness Training for Adolescents with Externalising Disorders and Their Parents." *Behavioural and Cognitive Psychotherapy* 36:1–17. doi: 10.1017/S1352465808004190.

Brown, K. W., and R. M. Ryan. 2003. "The Benefits of Being Present: Mindfulness and Its Role in Psychological Well-Being." *Journal of Personality and Social Psychology* 84:822–848. doi: 10.1037/0022-3514.84.4.822.

Burpee, L. C., and E. L. Lange. 2005. "Mindfulness and Marital Satisfaction." *Journal of Adult Development* 12:43–51. doi: 10.1007/s10804-005-1281-6.

Canny, G. O., and B. A. McCormick. 2008. "Bacteria in the Intestine, Helpful Residents or Enemies from Within." *Infection and Immunity* 76(8):3360-3373.

Carson, J. W., K. M. Carson, K. M. Gil, and D. H. Baucom. 2004. "Mindfulness-Based Relationship Enhancement." *Behavior Therapy* 35:471–494. doi: 10.1016/S0005-7894(04)80028-5.

Chong, C. S., M. Tsunaka, H. W. Tsang, E. P. Chan, and W. M. Cheung. 2011. Effects of Yoga on Stress Management in Healthy Adults: A Systematic Review." *Alternative Therapies in Health and Medicine* 17(1):32–38.

Crescentini, C., V. Capurso, S. Furlan, and F. Fabbro. 2016. "Mindfulness-Oriented Meditation for Primary School Children: Effects on Attention and Psychological Well-Being." *Frontiers in Psychology, 7,* 805. http://doi.org/10.3389/fpsyg.2016.00805

den Besten, Gijs., et al. 2013. "The Role of Short-Chain Fatty Acids in the Interplay between Diet, Gut Microbiota, and Host Energy Metabolism." *The Journal of Lipid Research* 54(9): 2325–2340.

Dumas, J. 2005. "Mindfulness-Based Parent Training: Strategies to Lessen the Grip of Automaticity in Families with Disruptive Children." *Journal of Clinical Child and Adolescent Psychology* 34:779–791. doi: 10.1207/s15374424jccp3404_20.

Duncan, L. G., J. D. Coatsworth, and M. T. Greenberg. 2009. "Pilot Study to Gauge Acceptability of a Mindfulness-Based, Family-Focused Preventive Intervention." *Journal of Primary Prevention* 30:605–618. doi: 10.1007/s10935-009-0185-9.

Gonzales, G. F., A. Cordova, K. Vega, A. Chung, A. Villeneuve, C. Gonez, and S. Castillo. 2002. "Effect of Lepidium Meyenii (MACA) on Sexual Desire and Its Absent Relationship with Serum Testosterone Levels in Adult Healthy Men." *Andrologia.* 34(6):367-72.

Hagen, I., and U. Nayar. 2014. "Yoga for Children and Young People's Mental Health and Well Being: Research Review and Reflection on the Mental Health Potentials of YOGA." *Front Psychiatry* 5:35. doi: 10.3389/fpsyt.2014.00035

Health Canada. 2012. "Natural Health Products Database: Maca." Accessed 5/3/17 from http://webprod.hc-sc.gc.ca/NHPID-BDIPSN/MONOREQ.DO?ID=1903&LANG=ENG

Hofmann, S. G., A. T. Sawyer, A. A. Witt, and D. Oh. 2010. "The Effect of Mindfulness-Based Therapy on Anxiety and Depression: A Meta-Analytic Review." *Journal of Consulting and Clinical Psychology* 78(2):169–183.

Jandhyala, S. M. 2015. "Role of the Normal Gut Microbiota." *World Journal of Gastroenterology.* Aug 7; 21(29): 8787–8803.

Jha, A., J. Krompinger, and M. Baime. 2007. "Mindfulness Training Modifies Subsystems of Attention." *Cognitive, Affective & Behavioural Neuroscience* 7:109–119. doi: 10.3758/CABN.7.2.109.

Kabat-Zinn, J. 1990. *Full Catastrophe Living: Using the Wisdom of Your Body and Mind to Face Stress, Pain, and Illness.* New York: Dell Publishing.

Kabat-Zinn, M., and J. Kabat-Zinn. 1997. *Everyday Blessings: The Inner Work of Mindful Parenting.* New York: Hyperion.

Kephart, H. 1916. *The Book of Camping and Woodcraft,* p. 196. New York: Windham Press.

Lazaridou, A., and C. Kalogianni. 2013. "Mindfulness and Sexuality." *Sexual and Relationship Therapy.* 28(1-2):29-38. doi: 10.1080/14681994.2013.773398.

Maranz, S., and Z. Wiesman. 2004. "Influence of Climate on the Tocopherol Content of Shea Butter." *J. Agric. Food Chem.* 52:2934–2937. doi: 10.1021/jf035194r.

Molajafar, H., S. M. Mousavi, R. Lotfi, S. M. Ghasemnejad, and M. Falah. 2015. "Comparing the Effectiveness of Mindfulness and Emotion Regulation Training in Reduction of Marital Conflicts." *Journal of Medicine and Life.* 8(2):111-116.

Morowitz, M. J., E. Carlisle, and J. C. Alverdy. 2011. "Contributions of Intestinal Bacteria to Nutrition and Metabolism in the Critically Ill." *Surgical Clinics of North America Jounral* 91(4):771–785.

National Institute of Mental Health. 2017. https://www.nimh.nih.gov/health/statistics/any-anxiety-disorder.shtml

Oluwaseyi Israel, M. 2014. "Effects of Topical and Dietary Use of Shea Butter on Animals." *American Journal of Life Sciences* 2(5):303-307. doi: 10.11648/j.ajls.20140205.18

Poplin, B., K. D'Anci, and I. Rosenberg. 2011. "Water, Hydration and Health." *Nutrition Reviews* 68(8):439–458. doi: 10.1111/j.1753-4887.2010.00304.x

Proctor, L. M. 2011. "The Human Microbiome Project in 2011 and Beyond." *Cell Host & Microbe* 10(4):287-91.

Rao, P., and S. Gan. 2014. "Cinnamon: A Multifaceted Medicinal Plant." *Evidence Based Complementary and Alternative Medicine.* doi: 10.1155/2014/642942

Reynolds, D. 2003. "Mindful Parenting: A Group Approach to Enhancing Reflective Capacity in Parents and Infants." *Journal of Child Psychotherapy* 29:357–374. doi: 10.1080/00754170310001625413.

Ross, A., E. Friedmann, M. Bevans, and S. Thomas. 2013. "National Survey of Yoga Practitioners: Mental and Physical Health Benefits." *Complementary Therapies in Medicine* 21:313–323.

Ross, A., and S. Thomas. 2010. "The Health Benefits of Yoga and Exercise: A Review of Comparison Studies." *Journal of Alternative and Complementary Medicine* 16:3–12.

Sandoval, M., et al. 2002. "Antioxidant Activity of the Cruciferous Vegetable Maca (Lepdidium Meyenii)." *Food Chemistry* 79, 207–213.

Sawyer, J. A. 2007. "Mindful Parenting, Affective Attunement, and Maternal Depression: A Call for Research." *Graduate Student Journal of Psychology* 9:3–9.

Schonert-Reichl, K. A., E. Oberle, M. S. Lawlor, D. Abbott, K. Thomson, T. F. Oberlander, A. Diamond. 2015. "Enhancing Cognitive and Social–Emotional Development Through a Simple-to-Administer

Mindfulness-Based School Program for Elementary School Children: A Randomized Controlled Trial." *Developmental Psychology* 51(1):52-66. doi: 10.1037/a0038454.

Siegel, D., T. P. Bryson. 2012. *The Whole Brain Child and Brain Storm: The Power and Purpose of the Teenage Brain.* New York: Bantam Books.

Singh, N., G. Lancioni, A. Winton, J. Singh, W. Curtis, R. Wahler et al. 2007. "Mindful Parenting Decreases Aggression and Increases Social Behavior in Children with Developmental Disabilities." *Behavior Modification* 31:749–771. doi: 10.1177/0145445507300924.

Singh, N., A. N. Singh, G. E. Lancioni, J. Singh, A. S. W. Winton, J. Singh et al. 2010. "Mindfulness Training for Parents and Their Children with ADHD Increases the Children's Compliance." *Journal of Child and Family Studies* 19:157–174. doi: 10.1007/s10826-009-9272-z.

Smalley, S. L., S. K. T. Loo, S. Hale, A. Shrestha, J. McGough, L. Flook et al. 2009. "Mindfulness and Attention Hyperactivity Disorder." *Journal of Clinical Psychology* 65:1087–1098. doi: 10.1002/jclp.20618.

Ursell, L. K., et al. 2012. "Defining the Human Microbiome." *Nutrition Reviews* 70(Suppl 1):S38–S44.

Vangalapati, M., N. Sree Satya, D. Surya Prakash, S. Avanigadda. 2012. "A Review on Pharmacological Activities and Clinical Effects of Cinnamon Species." *Research Journal of Pharmaceutical, Biological and Chemical Sciences* 3(1):653–663.

Vieten, D., and J. Astin. 2008. "Effects of Mindfulness-Based Intervention during Pregnancy on Prenatal Stress and Mood: Results of a Pilot Study." *Archives of Women's Mental Health* 11:67–74. doi: 10.1007/s00737-008-0214-3.

Wachs, K., and J. V. Cordova. 2007. "Mindful Relating: Exploring Mindfulness and Emotion Repertoires in Intimate Relationships. *Journal of Marital and Family Therapy* 33:464–481. doi: 10.1111/j.1752-0606.2007.00032.x.

Wahler, R., K. Rowinski, and K. Williams. 2008. "Mindful Parenting: An Inductive Search Process." In L. A. Greco and S. C. Hayes, editors. *Acceptance and Mindfulness Treatments for Adolescents and Children: A Practitioner's Guide.* Oakland, CA: New Harbinger Publications, pp. 217–235.

CPSIA information can be obtained
at www.ICGtesting.com
Printed in the USA
LVHW071941040419
613041LV00001B/1/P